Praise for *Stop, Ask*

Excellent leaders create conditions that advance and empower those around them, especially in times of uncertainty. In *Stop, Ask, Explore*, Joan P. Ball offers a field-tested framework and practical tools and approaches to help leaders—from first-time managers to C-suite executives—navigate change and equip their teams to overcome challenges in their presence, as well as their absence. FRANCES FREI, HARVARD BUSINESS SCHOOL PROFESSOR, THINKERS50 AWARD WINNER, AND CO-AUTHOR OF *UNLEASHED: THE UNAPOLOGETIC LEADER'S GUIDE TO EMPOWERING EVERYONE AROUND YOU*

So many books simply suggest that change is something we cope with, adjust to, or survive. This book does far more. Rather, in a wonderfully clear and gracious way, Joan P. Ball empowers us to find the power in flux. Once we've understood that possibility, we don't just cope. We're transformed. CAIT LAMBERTON, MBA, PHD, ALBERTO I. DURAN PRESIDENTIAL DISTINGUISHED PROFESSOR OF MARKETING AT THE WHARTON SCHOOL, UNIVERSITY OF PENNSYLVANIA

Creating a workplace where women of color can thrive requires a commitment to transformation in every part of the organization—and getting there means rethinking everything. In *Stop, Ask, Explore*, Joan P. Ball provides a framework that favors action and experimentation to navigate the messiness and uncertainty on the journey to genuine change. MINDA HARTS, WORKPLACE AND EQUITY CONSULTANT, PROFESSOR, AND AUTHOR OF *THE MEMO: WHAT WOMEN OF COLOR NEED TO KNOW TO SECURE A SEAT AT THE TABLE* AND *RIGHT WITHIN: HOW TO HEAL FROM RACIAL TRAUMA IN THE WORKPLACE*

A wonderful book asking profound, vital questions that will help propel us all to a better, more secure, more interesting, and successful life. TOM GOODWIN, CEO OF ALL WE HAVE IS NOW AND AUTHOR OF *DIGITAL DARWINISM: SURVIVAL OF THE FITTEST IN THE AGE OF BUSINESS DISRUPTION*

Joan P. Ball lit up a room of skeptical, hard-nosed engineers who aren't normally comfortable delving into soft skills. She used her authenticity, her wonderful energy, and her sense of humor to really reach them. I watched everyone's posture change during her presentation. Instead of sitting back with arms crossed, they were leaning forward and interacting with Joan as well as their peers. She gave them rich content that convinced them of the value of arming their teams with resilience, tools, and hope during a period that she so aptly described as "active waiting". KIM FURZER, CHIEF OF STAFF TO CIO, VERIZON MEDIA

All too often, disruption can drive one of two extreme reactions: either a deer in the headlights paralysis or knee-jerk response. *Stop, Ask, Explore* is the structured set of principles and fresh, practical tools that can finally equip leaders to take action that's truly effective in the face of disruption. It's the missing link in the path to get to the best "next". ANDREA KATES, PARTNER AT SUMA VENTURES AND AUTHOR OF *FIND YOUR NEXT: USING THE BUSINESS GENOME APPROACH TO FIND YOUR COMPANY'S NEXT COMPETITIVE EDGE* AND GET TO NEXT MASTERCLASS SERIES

Leadership of the recent past required unquestioned experts to drive productivity top-down through execution of well understood tasks in relative certainty. Leadership of the current requires humble, curious learners to inspire their people bottom-up to explore, to find, and to frame new challenges in a world of continuous change and uncertainty. *Stop, Ask, Explore* is not a "how to" book, because it acknowledges that we will not go back and our path forward is unclear. Since our path forward is yet to be forged, we need "learn to" guides that help us become comfortable with not knowing, exploring, and wayfinding. *Stop, Ask, Explore* is a book that clearly understands all this. From Joan P. Ball's deep research, we learn the power of self-reflection and self-awareness in establishing a new breed of leaders who can help lead us through ambiguity towards a better, more inclusive, and equitable future for all. HEATHER E. MCGOWAN, FUTURE OF WORK STRATEGIST, KEYNOTE SPEAKER, AND AUTHOR OF *THE ADAPTATION ADVANTAGE: LET GO, LEARN FAST, AND THRIVE IN THE FUTURE OF WORK*

Everybody has experienced the challenge of getting from "What now?" to "What's next?" In this wonderful book, told through compelling stories and backed by years of rigorous research, Joan P. Ball will help you do just that. This is so much more than a book to enhance your career. It will animate your life! I couldn't recommend it more highly. GREG SATELL, TRANSFORMATION AND CHANGE EXPERT, INTERNATIONAL KEYNOTE SPEAKER, AND BESTSELLING AUTHOR OF *CASCADES: HOW TO CREATE A MOVEMENT THAT DRIVES TRANSFORMATIONAL CHANGE*

STOP, ASK, EXPLORE

Learn to Navigate Change in Times of Uncertainty

Joan P. Ball

KoganPage

First published in Great Britain and the United States in 2022 by Kogan Page Limited

2nd Floor, 45 Gee Street
London
EC1V 3RS
United Kingdom

8 W 38th Street, Suite 902
New York, NY 10018
USA

4737/23 Ansari Road
Daryaganj
New Delhi 110002
India

www.koganpage.com

Kogan Page books are printed on paper from sustainable forests.

ISBNs
Hardback   978 1 3986 0562 6
Paperback   978 1 3986 0560 2
Ebook   978 1 3986 0561 9

British Library Cataloguing-in-Publication Data
A CIP record for this book is available from the British Library.

Library of Congress Control Number
2022002940

Typeset by Integra Software Services, Pondicherry
Print production managed by Jellyfish
Printed and bound by CPI Group (UK) Ltd, Croydon CR0 4YY

For Martin, Kelsey, Ian and Andrew—my partners
in wayfinding

"Explanations establish islands, even continents, of order and predictability. But these regions were first charted by adventurers whose lives are narratives of exploration and risk. They found them only by mythic journeys into the wayless open." — James P. Carse

Contents

Introduction

My father was thrilled the day I told him I had accepted an offer to be a communications manager at Consolidated Edison in New York City. It was 1994. I was a 28-year-old college graduate and a single mother with two kids aged five and six. He was sure accepting this job meant I'd finally get "back on track" in the wake of an unpredictable personal and professional journey through my early 20s.

"ConEd is a solid company with great benefits," he told me with a combination of celebration and relief. "You'll have this job for life."

Looking at this scene through 20th-century eyes, it's not surprising that he—a New York City fireman born in 1940 and raised in a working-class neighborhood in Brooklyn—believed that a position at a regulated utility company in New York City meant a stable and predictable path forward for me and my kids.

I did too.

None of us knew in the mid-1990s what changes were waiting just around the corner. Deregulation of industries, the dotcom boom (and bust), globalization, personal computing and the internet, mobile technology, social media, the rise of LGBTQ+ rights, 9/11, school shootings, the 2008 recession,

Ferguson, Black Lives Matter, MeToo, the Covid-19 pandemic. Despite the upheaval of the 1960s and '70s, many Americans in the late 20th century still embraced a collective naïveté about where a single mom with a degree in economics from a State university could go if she just worked hard, found the right job, the right partner, the right house, and lived the right kind of life. Many of us still embraced the hope (or the collective delusion) that things would get "back to normal" and that the post-WW2 American Dream was still ours to lose.

Despite starting our careers in a recession, those of us who came of age in the 1980s and '90s (Gen Xers if generations are your thing) benefited from that idealism. It kept us busy. It helped us focus. It provided a guiding framework for action—even when we chose to push up against it. We were like a group of passengers who survived a plane crash and landed in the middle of a dense forest. A ton of uncertainty, a dash of fear and despair, but still holding on to the hope that we would stumble upon a remote town or a search and rescue team.

But what happens when the rescue doesn't come—or to the people who never got a seat on the plane in the first place? What happens when the passengers are forced to accept that going back is not an option and the way forward is unclear? Xers were the first modern generational cohort to face that question, followed by the Millennials, and now Gens Z and A. Together with those who came before us, we're all now charged with learning new ways of being and doing work and life, on the fly in a shifting landscape. For me that's meant a half dozen jobs, two graduate degrees, a small business, and a (very!) surprising shift from traditional industry to academia—all since that "job for life" conversation with my father in 1994. And, while I've since gained some career stability as a tenured professor, researcher, writer and consultant, I'm confident that there are more surprises, opportunities and challenges in store as we all learn to adapt to new ideas and technologies that have yet to be imagined.

Learning to survive—and eventually flourish—in this new terrain will require us to accept that many of the strategies, tools and tactics that once provided comfort and guidance may no longer be relevant or helpful in this new environment. The 2020s are proving to be a time of wrestling and reckoning and renegotiation of what it means to live a good life, treat one another with dignity, share resources and influence, and collaborate with people who think, act and live differently than we do. We need to keep up with the compressed life cycle of skills and embrace lifelong learning or become obsolete. These are liminal times, and the future is uncharted territory. And learning to navigate uncharted territory requires a new relationship with uncertainty and change.

That's why the subtitle of the book says "learn to" rather than "how to." Exploring new ways to live, learn and lead in times of constant change is both exciting and daunting. It requires asking hard questions and a willingness to go beyond the familiar to find new, and sometimes surprising, answers. A committment to inquiry and discernment is necessary if we are to discover which frameworks, models and tools hold up in practice and what needs to be modified or adapted to meet the moment. The capacities, skills and practices we need to maintain our composure and thrive in changing circumstances are not developed from lists of how-tos or what-tos. Moreover, since every person and context is different, we need to train for many possible scenarios and develop our capacity to apply them (or get reinforcements) on the scene and in the moment. This is especially important in times when many of us feel overwhelmed with choices and change—real or perceived.

In the following pages I invite you to reimagine your relationship with uncertainty and change—even when it is frightening or frustrating. Not because it is comfortable, but because it is inevitable.

Rather than offering a prescriptive approach to navigating change, *Stop, Ask, Explore* invites you to consider the benefits of learning to *stop* in order to gather the resources you need to acknowledge and accept when change feels threatening and make space for learning. Then, once settled into a dispassionate curiosity, we are more able to *ask* how best to engage these questions for yourself by considering the particular resources you need to respond (rather than react) to life in this environment, and then *explore* new possibilities in a way that takes into consideration who you are, where you are, and where you hope to go. It is a book about growing capacity to face uncertainty head on and learning to flourish when interruptions and disruptions throw us for a loop.

This book evolved from nearly a decade of research into one simple (but not so simple) question: what prevents talented, ambitious and change-minded people from responding well to uncertainty and finding new ways to live meaningful and impactful lives? My curiosity about these questions was piqued about 10 years ago, when I noticed a viral "stuckness" among my business students as they sought to cross the threshold from school to work. It was the early 2010s, when the generational cohort we call Millennials (or Gen Y) was coming of age and 20-somethings entering the workforce at the time were routinely portrayed as lacking the skills and motivation to move into adulthood. Research reports with titles like *Failure to Launch: Structural shift and the new lost generation* (Carnevale et al, 2013) and *A Rising Share of Adults Live in Their Parents' Home* (Fry, 2013) described the challenges that both blue- and white-collar workers faced as they attempted to start their careers in the wake of the 2008 financial crisis. The theory of emerging adulthood, a relatively new research stream in developmental psychology at the time, called for acknowledgment of the 20s as a new life stage in industrialized countries due to a variety of factors, including shifting cultural norms regarding marriage, family, and other traditional markers of "growing up" (Arnett, 2000).

At the time, many people scoffed at the idea of emerging adulthood, preferring to embrace a narrative that young people were simply lazy, entitled and content to live off their parents. This tension was fueled by hundreds—if not thousands—of click-bait titles that blamed hover-parenting and trophy culture for a generation lost on the road to adulthood, more than happy to benefit from the comforts of their parents' homes and enjoy a delayed start. While this stereotype was born in a critique of young people in the upper socioeconomic classes, it settled into the public imagination as a Millennial phenomenon that crossed class, ethnic, racial and national boundaries.

But I observed something very different in my undergraduate and graduate business students. Many were ambitious and hard working. They were more than eager to set out on their own, but felt hamstrung by debt, a tight job market and the rising cost of housing in many cities across the globe. This made sense on one level. The early 2010s economy was still reeling from the 2008 economic crisis, and the transition into the workforce was not easy. Yet, Millennials were not the first cohort of young people to enter adulthood in trying times—and events like the Covid-19 pandemic make it clear that they will not be the last. But something about the experience facing this group of graduates felt different.

I recall sitting in my office across the desk from a young man as he told me how trapped (but grateful) he felt living with his parents. "I want to go out on my own," he told me through tears, "but I just can't see a way forward from here." The more I poked and prodded and gathered the stories of these young people, the more I began to suspect that there was something about this stuckness and the resulting "failure to launch" that the existing analysis was missing.

And it wasn't just my students.

As I expanded the inquiry to more established professionals and their teams in their 20s, 30s, 40s and beyond, I noted a similar stuckness in people of different age cohorts, life stages, socioeconomic and cultural circumstances. I saw it in emerging leaders charting new career paths and seeking new ways to integrate rather than balance their work and life. I observed it in my work with the Center for Social Innovation in New York City where more than 300 small- to medium-size social enterprises were reimagining the social contract and exploring the intersection of commerce and human connection worldwide. I saw it in the teams and departments I worked with in legacy business organizations as they sought innovative ways to adapt to changes sparked by the effect of new technologies and an increasingly uncertain future of work. I saw it in professional women in my field from across the globe.

Rather than study these challenges from a distance, I facilitated transition workshops, which led to more formal participatory action research with multi-year cohorts and one-on-one engagements in established organizations and startups. This led to multi-day retreats for emerging and established leaders, small business owners, community leaders and educators, where I learned more about the challenges people faced as they wrestled with change and uncertainty in their professional and personal lives. In every setting, despite the variety of contexts, educational backgrounds and socioeconomic resources, these engagements led me to smart, ambitious and talented people who searched for words to describe this... something... they couldn't put their fingers on that kept getting in their way or holding them back.

As I continued to explore, I noticed new language emerging in popular culture to describe people having trouble finding their way at points of transition. Among the early career cohorts, terms like "quarter-life crisis" and "adulting" were coined to describe a shift in how people in their 20s and 30s were approaching professional and personal aspirations and commitments (Robinson, 2015). In mid-life, "sandwich" or "panini" generation were used to describe the pressures facing families in their 40s raising young children while caring for aging parents (Williams, 2004). The term "third act" emerged to describe elders exploring what it takes to live and thrive for decades past traditional retirement age (Black, 2020). The challenges of moving through life stages is nothing new, of course. So why are so many people having so much trouble navigating them? Robert Frost's 1915 poem, *The Road Not Taken*, hints at an answer.

Picture Frost standing at a turning point, sorry that he has to choose one of two roads before him rather than take them both. "And be one traveler, long I stood," Frost (1915) writes as he peers down the two roads hoping to see something that might help him to decide which road he wants to take. He eventually makes a choice, but the turning point offers him both a sense of opportunity and uncertainty that points to a quaint early 20th-century version of FOMO.

But what if Frost were writing in the 2020s?

Equipped with groundbreaking technology, shifting cultural norms, new and evolving community and family structures, and emerging ways of living and working, the 21st-century traveler faces countless possible roads to enter a shape-shifting wood. The sheer quantity of choices about where to live, how to live and why we do it means we're often paving our own roads while we're traveling on them. More like bushwhacking into uncharted territory than choosing a road more or less traveled. This new terrain offers countless exciting new opportunities for people from all backgrounds to chart new paths that were once impossible to imagine. At the same time, this freedom to work, and live, in new ways can be destabilizing, disorienting and overwhelming. If standing on the threshold of two possible options gave Frost's traveler pause in the early 20th century, it's no wonder we feel stuck, lost and confused when we face ours. I've come to believe that this is the piece we're missing about the Millennial failure to launch and other examples of stuckness when facing uncertain transitions. We've underestimated what it takes to equip ourselves and others to navigate in uncharted territory and the emotional, physical and social toll it takes when we feel under-equipped to do it.

It is through this lens that I offer *Stop, Ask, Explore*. Not as a solution, but as a call to inquiry, exploration and the equipping of a community of wayfinders who can navigate without a map or compass. This is a practical book that is rooted in theory and research conducted with individuals, teams and organizations in transition. The content is presented in three main sections that are bookended by two chapters that set the stage for readers to embark on a wayfinding journey, individually or with a team.

Part One draws from self-regulation, resilience, curiosity and conceptual metaphor theories and presents frameworks, principles and practices drawn from ongoing participatory action research. New concepts including dispassionate curiosity and active resilience are introduced as routes to help temper the threat response and open transitional learning space in the face of uncertain transitions.

Part Two introduces frameworks built upon hope theory designed to prompt self-awareness, self-direction and sensemaking as routes to inquiry in transitional learning spaces.

Part Three introduces the experiment design canvas, and the learn, discern, choose, confirm framework for transitioning out of liminal learning spaces. Detailed lists of resources and references are provided at the end of the book for readers who are interesting in reading more about the theory behind the practice. Stories and anecdotes are based upon real people who have engaged with the frameworks, principles and practices in a variety of settings and contexts. Some go by their given names. Others are pseudonyms and their stories have been amended to protect their anonymity.

In any case, the book is designed to be a practical guide to learning to flourish when living in the liminal, whether that means changes at the society level or the uncertainty that comes from a change in your family, your job, your health or your business. It is my hope that the work will provide an artifact to support further participatory action research with new communities and a support for people to help one another to learn to navigate change in uncertain times.

In the beginning of his seminal book *Story*, Robert McKee writes, "A rule says, 'You must do it this way.' A principle says, 'This works... and has through all remembered time'." (McKee, 1999). In the pages that follow, you will find no rules for what it takes to learn to navigate change in uncertain times. To offer a prescription for adapting to an unfolding reality that is beyond our imagining would be at best unhelpful and at worst malpractice. Instead, I invite you to consider the value of pausing, asking good questions, and exploring possibilities to help you to make sense of how you can learn to the changing terrain of 21st-century life. I invite you to recognize that quick decisions are not always good decisions, and to see the value of opening up space and time for reflection, sensemaking, discernment and wayfinding for you and those your serve. Here's hoping you will find your way—or, as my friend and colleague a.m. Bhatt likes to say, for your way to find you.

CHAPTER ONE

What Now? Moments and navigating uncharted territory

It is time now to explore the creative potential of interrupted and conflicted lives, where energies are not narrowly focused or permanently pointed toward a single ambition. These are not lives without commitments, but lives in which commitments are continually refocused and redefined.

MARY CATHERINE BATESON

I met Ashley Rigby at a mentoring event in New York City. We found each other at the refreshment table in the impeccably designed offices of a 100+-year-old furniture design firm with showrooms across the globe. Ashley filled a small plate with fruit and cheese and poured a sparkling water as she told me that she was a regional sales manager with the company and a mentor co-hosting the event. Over the 10-minute break between sessions I learned that she was a rising star at the company who had captured the attention of senior leadership. I also learned that, despite having ample opportunity for promotion and professional development, she was thinking about leaving to follow a dream.

"I started something with my mother and my sister," she told me. "A side gig really, but I'd love it to become something more." She went on to describe a community-based organization called Jam Program that they had designed together to provide space for women to network and share resources. Pilot events in Brooklyn, NY and Hartford, CT were already gaining momentum with cross-generational cohorts of professional women, and Ashley was confident that leaving her position and focusing on Jam Program full-time was necessary to take the project to the next level. It was apparent even in the short time we had together that Ashley and her partners had the vision, skills and capacity to make the new venture work. Perhaps even more importantly, the ambition and motivation were there. She was clearly hungry to do something meaningful, something with purpose, something that fulfilled her desire to be of service to others and to herself.

But she was also conflicted.

I watched the expression on her face toggle between excitement and hesitation as she described competing priorities and commitments at the intersection of a promising career, a high-potential passion project, and a very active family life with her husband and two young children. While she was more than capable of making tough decisions and following through on them, she was struggling to find a way to bring her best in three domains at once. Despite feeling stuck, Ashley was confident that she'd figure something out eventually. In the meantime, the plan was to keep her head down and juggle the job, the side hustle and family responsibilities until she could see a path forward—even though she knew her current pace was not sustainable. We set a time to grab a coffee the following week.

I've heard stories like Ashley's hundreds of times, in different forms and for as many reasons, as an educator and in my research and consulting practice. Whether I'm working with college students, helping early- to mid-career professionals to integrate their professional and personal priorities, or equipping established leaders and their teams to imagine the future of work, a common thread runs through their varied experiences. Regardless of the particulars, even the most educated, talented and experienced people can (and often do) get stuck when they stand on the threshold of a professional or personal transition.

Who among us hasn't, like Ashley, found ourselves operating at an unsustainable pace without a clear sense of how to lighten the load? Or received that text, call or email with news—good or bad—that upends our plans and forces us to reconsider the path we're on? From high-stakes disruptions like job transitions, to the daily challenges of dealing with a difficult co-worker, situations that scuttle our plans or challenge our intentions are an inevitable part of professional and personal life. And, while many of us may feel we have a gift for avoiding unwelcome surprises, even the most foreseeable life changes—like graduations, marriages, children and job promotions—can ignite the need to rethink how we live and work. Yet, even if we acknowledge that "the only constant is change"

Regardless of the particulars, even the most educated, talented and experienced people can (and often do) get stuck when they stand on the threshold of an uncertain professional or personal transition.

and accept that we need to "get comfortable being uncomfortable," most of us devote very little time or attention to the practice of preparing ourselves to navigate uncertain transitions. Though it's not for a lack of trying.

Visit any large bookstore in person or online and you'll find thousands of titles, that have sold millions of copies, on the topic of change. In the same way that most people know they should eat well and exercise to keep in shape, it's not news to anyone reading this book that the world is changing, and we need to build new capacities and skills to keep up. Perhaps you've already committed to having a growth mindset, building new skills and capacities, improving your EQ and becoming more empathetic, vulnerable and adaptive in your professional and personal life. Unfortunately, if you're like most people, you live somewhere in the gap between these ideals and reality—and the distance between can feel like a chasm. Add an interruption or disruption to the mix and we find ourselves in an all-too-common conundrum: drowning in ideals, frameworks and change management approaches yet feeling perpetually under-equipped when we face uncertain transitions.

Too many tools, not enough practice

In an era where we've decided that more data and information is better, the sheer quantity of change-related tools and tactics can actually hinder efforts to navigate change, especially in times of uncertainty. In fact, attempts to apply one-size-fits-all solutions to nuanced challenges in shifting contexts can actually contribute to rather than alleviate the destabilization, disorientation and stuckness we feel when we face disruption. This is not as counterintuitive as it may seem. In the same way that a building contractor doesn't use every tool in the truck for every job, we don't need *all of the tools* at our disposal to navigate every part of every uncertain transition. Identifying the *appropriate tools* for the circumstances and engaging them in helpful ways, when they're needed, is a skill we rarely discuss or practice. As a result, we often confuse having a tool with knowing how to use it in practice.

I see this principle in action every time a person shakes a mobile phone at someone and says, "You have all of the world's information at your fingertips, why don't you know how to _____?" Assuming that access to technology means knowing how to apply the information you find there in context is like stepping into the lobby of The Library of Congress in

Washington, DC (the largest in the world) and expecting to be able to apply the content in the 170 million items in your day-to-day life. Unfortunately, much of our education, training and professional development operates on this assumption. That having access to information about change and uncertainty means that we actually know how to make sense of it and are able to draw useful insights that we can apply easily in dynamic circumstances.

As a result, we spend tons of time, energy and money on *learning about* change rather than developing consistent and sustainable practices and approaches to help us *apply what we learn* in context.

Our relationship with speed and decisiveness may be partially to blame for this. In a world where faster frequently means better and efficiency is glorified, intentionally making time and space to stop, ask good questions and explore possible routes forward when we face uncertain transitions is viewed as a luxury at best, and indecision at worst. As a result, we often make quick decisions with partial information about situations that are new and emerging—then wonder why we feel lost in transition or wind up in places we never wanted to go as people we never expected (or wanted) to be. Ashley and her decision about whether to remain at her job or leave and focus on her startup provides a perfect example.

We spend tons of time, energy and money on learning about change rather than developing consistent and sustainable practices and approaches to help us apply what we learn in context.

We had a long coffee a week after that event, and it was clear that Ashley would likely benefit from carving out time to reflect on her work situation more deeply. I invited her to join me for a solo retreat. The experience involves a few days of completely unstructured time alone in a comfortable loft space. No mealtimes. No workshops. No massages or meditation classes. No alarms. No agenda. Just space, time and two three-hour conversations—one at the beginning and one at the end to help retreat participants to enter and exit the space with some intention (or not). There is no prescription for what people discuss in these conversations or how they spend their time between them. My only request (and it is only a request) is that visitors set aside their usual work and make space to step out of their normal routines. Most report that it is the first unscheduled time they've spent in years—and, for some, the first in their adult life.

Ashley, like so many others, arrived for her visit ready for a highly productive weekend. We laughed together as I pointed out the irony of showing up with an open canvas bag filled with more than a dozen leadership and personal development books. Over the course of our first three-hour conversation, it became clear that she had read everything there was to read about change, transition and building a successful career. Yet, when faced with the challenge of deciding how best to apply that learning to make sense of her particular situation, the "how to" and "what to" models fell short. I listened closely as she described her happy home, her love for her work at the design company, a growing dissatisfaction with her role there, and her deep desire to build Jam Program into something more. When she finished, I asked a clarifying question.

"Are leaving your job or staying at the company your only choices?"

She responded like most people do when I pose this sort of question: with a list of constraints and issues that completely justified her working theory that there were only two paths forward. She could stay at her primary job and keep the new business small or leave her job and focus on the passion project full-time. "Perhaps you're right," I pressed. "Tell me about how you identified those two options."

Despite having thought about it deeply, she could not articulate how she'd arrived at these two choices. She talked about logic and common sense as she described the unconscious process she'd used to consider what was possible. We discussed the importance of considering less obvious potential choices, and I invited her to consider using her time on retreat to better understand her current context before deciding what might come next. I left her with large sketch pads, a white board, sticky notes, markers and a few prompts to help her get whatever was on her mind out of her head and in front of her. "Forget the books," I suggested. "Acknowledge that you stand at the threshold of a space between What Now? and whatever comes next that is ripe with creative possibility if you allow it to be."

The space between What Now? and what comes next

It's important to note here that I didn't know Ashley very well at the time and I had little context for what she wanted and what might be best for her career, her family or her life. I had no insight into whether leaving her job was the right move for her and, to be quite candid, I didn't care. Guiding her in a particular direction—toward greater success or a higher salary or greater wellbeing and slowing down—was not my aim. My hope for her, and for anyone reading this book, is to build upon what Mary Catherine Bateson wrote so elegantly in the quote at the beginning of the chapter and help people at every life stage to recognize that the uncertain transitions we face across the span of our interrupted and conflicted lives offer tremendous creative potential to refocus and redefine our commitments.

The uncertain transitions we face across the span of our interrupted and conflicted lives offer tremendous creative potential to reflect, refocus and redefine our commitments.

And yet, rather than respond to that creative potential as an invitation, we often view interruptions and disruptions as a threat. These What Now? Moments, which I define as *any interruption or disruption that causes a person to feel lost, uncertain, disoriented or stuck in the face of an uncertain transition*, can spark uncomfortable thoughts, incendiary emotions and knee-jerk reactions, especially if we don't have a clear and immediate sense of how best to respond. That's why I believe that acknowledging the inevitability of What Now? Moments, and developing the practices we need to prepare ourselves to navigate them in professional and personal contexts, is a 21st-century imperative. So, what gets in the way?

Interruptions, disruptions and the What Now? Moment

Interruptions and disruptions come in many shapes and sizes. Internally in the form of our thoughts, feelings or aspirations— or exernally in the form of expected and unexpected situations that keep us from doing what we plan, when and how we plan it. As illustrated in Figure 1.1, they can have a spiky side, like when we lose a job unexpectedly or are forced to deal with a chronic illness. But they can also emerge when things go our way, like when we're offered a big promotion or get engaged to the love of our life. In any case, interruptions and disruptions capture our attention and can be destabilizing.

Of course, not all interruptions and disruptions are destabilizing. Sometimes the way forward is clear and we are able to recover easily and move on quickly. When a way forward is less clear, however, we can feel lost or unsettled. This can compound feelings of uncertainty, disorientation, distraction and despair and result in intense, incendiary emotions.

There is ample research to suggest that it is possible to temper our incendiary emotions if we are properly resourced, and that doing so can be beneficial in a variety of ways. (see Appendix A).

So, why don't we do it?

FIGURE 1.1   What Now? Moments

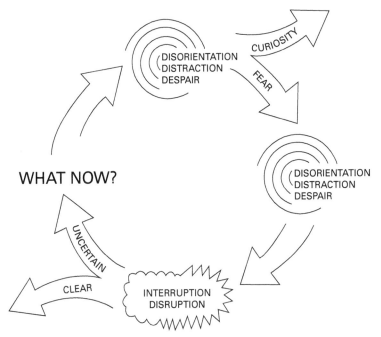

QUESTIONS FOR REFLECTION

When is the last time you faced a What Now? Moment?

What was your initial response?

Did you take immediate action? Avoid? Other?

If you had paused and taken more time before acting—whether it be a week, a day or even just an hour—how might you have responded differently to the situation?

"There is no time!" and "You don't understand what we're up against!" are two of the most common reasons people give to justify succumbing to threat reactions with quick decisions and bold responses rather than making time and space for inquiry in the face of a What Now? Moment. Inquiry requires shifting from a *knowing orientation* to a *learning orientation*, which is counterintuitive in environments where decisiveness is rewarded. Navigating the uncharted territory that emerges from a What Now? Moment requires a willingness to adapt to the needs of the context—with or without ample data—which can feel risky when applied in systems where certainty and clarity are considered leadership virtues. Fortunately, we can draw upon other contexts, such as emergency services, to model how inquiry and exploration can co-exist with precision and expertise in the face of uncertainty, even when we feel time compressed.

Stop, drop and roll

As the child of a New York City firefighter, I was raised with fire safety as a front-of-mind priority. I knew which route I would take if the house went up in flames, how to best evacuate from my second-floor bedroom, to crawl on the floor to avoid smoke, and to "stop, drop and roll" if my clothing were ever on fire. I was also taught that whatever I learned would need to be abandoned if the route I chose was blocked or if I found myself in an unexpected situation. "Fire is unpredictable," my father would tell us. "The best you can do is create a plan, but also be ready for anything." Years later I worked for Consolidated Edison, a large electric utility company in New York City, and was deeply involved in emergency planning efforts at the Indian Point Nuclear Power Plant. Like those childhood exercises, we developed elaborate emergency management plans for the plant and surrounding 50 miles. We held days-long drills with detailed scenarios for evacuating millions of people if there were an event at the plant. My father's words were true in that case as well. The best you can do is create a plan, but also be ready for anything.

The more I learn about how people respond to What Now? Moments, the more I think about my father's words and my experiences with emergency planning. There is an uncanny similarity between the ways people respond to incendiary emotions when a What Now? Moment throws them into uncharted territory, and how people respond to other types of emergencies. Fear. Panic. Fight. Flight. Freeze. That's why, whether it's a fire drill or learning to stop, drop and roll, we practice *before* the fire starts so we're as well equipped as we can be in the heat of the moment.

What is stop, drop and roll?

For those who are not familiar with what I mean when I say *"stop, drop and roll"*, the term was introduced in the 1970s as a fire safety public service announcement in the United States. The reason for the campaign is terrifying. A cutting-edge fabric technology—polyester—was used in a popular nightshirt that would catch fire easily. Despite a 1953 regulation to ban the fabric, polyester stayed on the market and a public service announcement became necessary to help people know what to do when their clothing caught on fire. Non-flammable fabric is now a thing, but this simple framework is still taught in schools in many countries across the globe, so kids are prepared to respond well in the face of a fire emergency of this sort. Without it, people are more likely to follow the impulse to run than they are to stop and drop to the ground to put out the flames. The same can be true in the context of preparing to navigate change in times of uncertainty.

When a What Now? Moment sparks our threat response, a similar mantra can remind us that we can stop to self-regulate, ask relevant questions and explore possibilities rather than react impulsively to unfamiliar or threatening circumstances. In doing so, we have a greater likelihood of moving from a fear-based, knee-jerk reaction to a curious and thoughtful response to changing circumstances. It stands to reason that, in the same way that we prepare ourselves in early childhood for how best to respond to fire and other emergencies, we can prepare ourselves for life's inevitable What Now? Moments. Enter *stop, ask, explore.*

Stop, ask and explore

The nature of any given What Now? Moment varies widely, but one thing is common among them—when they spark our threat response, everyone panics. Even emergency responders and others who are trained to operate well in danger. In fact, professionals who operate in dangerous environments learn to temper the threat response as part of their training. No matter our level of experience, we are all subject to physical and emotional responses to uncertainty that we perceive to be threatening. This may land uncomfortably—especially for people who are used to putting out "fires" at home and at work on a regular basis. But even the most seasoned among us can get caught up in our own incendiary emotional and physical responses at the point of impact of a What Now? Moment. In this way, our initial reaction to a What Now? Moment is like reacting to a house on fire. If we can condition ourselves to *stop, ask and explore*, we can find more creative and context-appropriate responses to uncertain transitions.

Stop: settle incendiary emotions

If we succumb to our incendiary emotions, we may enter a *fear loop* (see Figure 1.1), which is *when the incendiary emotions compound feelings of threat, disorientation, distraction and despair, leading to further interruption and disruption in the face of uncertainty and change.* By pausing to acknowledge and accept when we are reacting to threat rather than responding to the disruption, we can make space to understand what has changed and how best to respond. This might involve not reacting immediately to the excitement of being offered a promotion or the concern about losing a job and creating space to consider the implications before choosing a path forward.

Ask: practice dispassionate curiosity and open transitional learning space

If we intentionally inquire about our new circumstances and open space for learning, we may enter a *curiosity loop,* which is *when tempering the threat response at a point of interruption or disruption is followed by intentional inquiry that leads to increased feelings of agency, hope and motivation.* This *dispassionate curiosity* can be a countermeasure to falling into the fear loop when we face a What Now? Moment (more on this in Chapter 2). This might involve considering new questions, like: What will the promotion mean beyond money and title? What about the level of responsibility? Does it work with other areas in your life? Will it lead in the direction you hope your career might go?

Explore: create opportunities for learning in action

If the inquiry suggests the position is right for you or leads to a clear path forward after the job loss, take the position or move on to a new one, and good luck! No need to explore beyond that return to clarity. If the inquiry raises new and important questions, there are many ways to explore new possibilities. This may involve taking the position on a trial basis to determine if it is the right fit or considering a new industry or cross-training in the wake of a job loss. More on exploration in later chapters.

In any case, the prompt to stop, ask, explore reminds us that we are capable of more than an incendiary reaction when we face What Now? Moments. In Ashley's case, she confirmed by the end of her retreat that she loved the company where she worked and valued the time she'd spent there. She also recognized that she could only stay there long-term if she was involved in work that was more aligned with her desire to engage in community building through her startup. She left at the end of the weekend not having chosen either of the two paths she had believed to be the only ones before her at the outset of the retreat. Instead, she decided to propose a new role for herself that would serve both the needs of the company and her desire to pursue her passion project. By the end of that same week, she called me. "This is why we hired you," her boss had told her at the end of a fruitful discussion about her future at the company. "To come up with ideas like this." By making space and taking time to consider new possibilities beyond the binary stay or go, Ashley opened new doors for herself that continue to create exciting opportunities at the design firm and beyond.

Of course, it could have gone the other way for Ashley. Pausing to temper incendiary emotions and to make space between What Now? and what comes next is not a magic bullet. Pursuing new possibilities does not always result in the answers we want—but it does give us what we need to make more informed choices rather than speeding through interruptions and disruptions without consideration. This creates room to reflect on the implications of the change or how it might affect who we are, where we are and where we hope to be. It is also a way to acknowledge that, despite all of the "rethink," "reimagine" and "innovate" rhetoric that is popular today, most of us (I include myself in this category) remain novices in the art of finding our way when the way forward is unclear. *Stop, ask, explore* is not a cure for that ailment. Instead, it is a prompt for all of us to acknowledge that What Now? Moments are inevitable, and that we can develop practices and approaches to help us learn to carve new paths forward when navigating uncharted territory in response to change.

So, please don't engage this work to find your superpowers or add another checklist of activities to your already busy schedule. Instead, consider this an invitation for you, your team, your organization or even your family to consider how you deal with change and what it might take to gather the resources you need to be better prepared to respond well to your next What Now? Moment. Or, if you're facing a What Now? Moment right now, it is an opportunity to engage with change in new ways and to develop new practices that make sense for you and your situation. And finally, it is an invitation for all of us to get better at helping one another to navigate the uncertain transitions we will face together as we reimagine and reshape our organizations, communities and lives built for the pursuit of human flourishing in the 21st century.

So, as you engage with the content of this book, I ask nothing more of you than to become willing to enter the unknown and learn what opportunities exist there—even when we have no true north, compass or maps upon which to rely. Then, as we enter this transitional learning space, let's acknowledge that we are neither doomed nor can we rely on the magic of positive thinking to navigate change in uncertain times. Instead, we can learn to accept that operating in uncharted territory may feel uncomfortable and that the terrain might not feel accommodating. But this is the straw we've pulled as human beings born in this time in the place where we find ourselves. So, like other humans born before us to uncertain times, we need to examine ourselves and determine how we want to live, what meaning we hope to bring to bear on the circumstances we're facing, and what it will mean to live well together in uncertain times.

So, What Now?

TAKEAWAYS

- What Now? Moments are inevitable, so we need to prepare ourselves to navigate in the uncharted territory between What Now? and what comes next.

- Learning to orient ourselves when we feel lost in uncharted territory is a 21st-century imperative.

- We can improve our relationship with change and uncertainty, but it takes willingness to learn, attention and practice.

PART ONE

Stop

A note to the reader as you begin 'Stop'

If you are skeptical of stopping in the face of change and uncertainty, then you are entering into this section of the book with just the right attitude. For a variety of conscious and unconscious reasons, pausing in the face of uncertainty and change can feel counterintuitive—even dangerous. In this section I invite you to explore the relationship that you and those you engage with professionally and personally have with uncertainty, transitions and change. These What Now? Moments are inevitable, so understanding who we are and where we hope to go at points of inflection is a practice we need to cultivate in ourselves and others in times of persistent change. I hope you will take advantage of the prompts, mark up the book, and engage with the work in a way that allows you to be challenged and to challenge back. This is your journey—and I'm honored to be part of it.

Here's to a healthy pause,

Joan

CHAPTER TWO

Don't follow your passion

Dispassionate curiosity and active resilience

"Imagine you're sitting on this beach." I'm standing beneath a floor-to-ceiling video screen projecting a loop of an empty beach and the blue sky on a beautiful sunny day. The sound of waves lapping on clean white sand fills the room where a group of social enterprise leaders are gathered for a workshop at the Centre for Social Innovation in New York City. I offer a series of prompts—pausing briefly between each to make space for the participants to imagine themselves in the scenario.

"What do you see?" I ask them.

"Is anyone there with you?"

"How do you feel?"

Whether it's due to the calming sound of the waves, the clear blue sky on the horizon, or their desire to place themselves in the relaxing scene, the responses start slowly and gradually pick up steam. Some participants imagine beaches filled with colorful umbrellas, cool drinks and island music. Others a quiet place where they can enjoy some solitude. As the stories become more detailed and personal, people loosen up and begin to have a little fun with it. They smile and laugh together, comparing notes about hanging out with friends and family or much-needed rest and relaxation. Despite being strangers only minutes earlier, momentum builds, and ideas start to flow effortlessly. Individuals come together to combine experiences and weave stories of larger beach parties.

I give them some time to enjoy each other and their faux beach vacations before I change the image on the screen. The horizon is the same, but in the second scenario a nearly capsized sailboat can be seen at the center of the image. The sea is calm, and the boat appears to be recently abandoned. "Now," I say. "Imagine you're sitting on the same beach, but you just survived a boating accident. You're soaking wet, full of sand and feeling winded after swimming to shore. What Now?"

I've run this exercise with hundreds of people—from students to leaders and their teams—and the results are remarkably similar. The transition from playful imagining to hard-nosed problem solving happens in an instant. People who were laughing together a moment earlier shift their tone and body language to postures that say, "Let's get down to business."

Unlike the generative, upbeat conversations that tend to bubble up from the first beach fantasy prompt, the shipwreck conversations generally provoke the creation of small subgroups who develop concrete plans with surprising speed. Some even take on a mildly combative tone as they debate which approach to take in the face of a fictional What Now? Moment.

Without any guidance beyond the initial prompts, two primary groups tend to emerge in the shipwreck scenario. I call them the rescuers and the survivalists. The rescuers favor taking immediate steps to get off the island. "We should draw a big SOS in the sand or swim out to the boat to see if there are flares, or start a signal fire," they say, as they consider how best to connect with a passing ship or plane passing overhead. "No, no," the survivalists tell them. "We need to build a shelter and find food and water before the sun goes down." The more time I allow for this part of the exercise, the more assured the two factions become that their approach is the right one and the more animated they are in their defense of their chosen position. As individual and group confidence grows, the sense that the others simply don't see the (completely fictional) situation clearly tends to emerge.

As the debate continues, a third, less cohesive, group of people emerges organically—the disengaged. These people quietly pick up their phones, excuse themselves to go to the bathroom, or otherwise pull out of the exercise. Some chat together, while others sit alone doing other work or watching the scene unfold from across the room. I walk around and ask them individually or in small groups how they would respond to the scenario. Most say that they'd wait to see how things played out and follow the group decision. Others say they would have already left the beach by themselves or with a small group to explore the rest of the island. Eventually, I break into the debate between the rescuers and survivalists to ask a clarifying question:

"What if there's a resort on the other side of the island?"

The humble pause that follows is simply delightful. People who were certain of their view of the situation a moment before smile sheepishly as they look around at one another. Most are quick to admit that in their haste they jumped to solution-finding before thinking through the problem (although, a few always blame the scenario and my "unclear instructions"). The disengaged crowd finally speaks up—often glibly—saying they would have already found the resort and been on the deck with a cool drink waiting for the others to figure it out.

QUESTION FOR REFLECTION

What was your first thought about the best response to the beach scenario?

The point of the exercise becomes clear as the larger groups admit that they jumped the gun. Most smile and say I "got" them. Wherever they land, the group is now primed to discuss the potential perils of reacting to disruption quickly, without thinking. We discuss how we often perceive What Now? Moments as a threat that can prompt a fight (take steps to survive), flight (seek rescue) or freeze (opt out) reaction. The "stop" in *stop, ask, explore* prompts us to acknowledge that initial reaction, and points to the value of developing a practice that helps to create space between our first, often emotional, reaction to threat and a response that is informed by both our emotions AND our circumstances—even when time is of the essence.

Of course, that can be easier said than done.

Practicing stop in a world that wants go

"I don't have time to stop!"

"I don't need to stop!"

"I'm already stuck and you're asking me to stop—I need to figure out how to get going!"

These are three of the most common reactions I observe when I invite people to consider intentionally stopping at the point of impact of a What Now? Moment. The exclamation points are not for effect. The call to stop is alarming for many people. It sparks reactions that lead people to wonder if I'm either naive or delusional by even hinting at the suggestion. How could I possibly think that to stop could be the right option for their situation? Implied (and sometimes stated) in this response is that I have no idea what I'm talking about or what they are going through. If I did, they tell me, I wouldn't dare to think they have the option, interest, or necessity to stop.

You may be thinking the same thing yourself as you read this.

Neuroscientists, psychologists, and others who plumb the depths of the human brain to understand how we tick are making remarkable strides in learning about what happens in our minds and bodies when we face a perceived threat. We know more than ever about the brain: which parts are active, what responses lead to more or less activity, the involvement of the nervous system, and the ways our bodies drive our thoughts, and our thoughts drive our bodies (Hartley et al, 2010). Yet, this emerging understanding of the physiology and psychology of perceived threat does little to help us with the practical matter of acknowledging that, when we're presented with uncertain circumstances, even the most experienced and well-trained among us can default to knee-jerk reactions.

These instinctive reactions can be helpful sometimes. Like when we pull our hand away when it gets too close to a hot stove, or we rush a child to the hospital when they break their arm playing on the playground. It makes sense to take these actions because we know that burns are worth avoiding and that broken bones need to be set. But what happens when our past experiences don't fully inform our understanding of future challenges and we need to adapt to an uncertain environment? How can we act quickly to bring both our past experience and the

When we're presented with uncertain circumstances, even the most experienced and well-trained among us can default to knee-jerk reactions.

emerging reality of a changing situation to bear in a way that moves from reaction to response? Let's consider these questions through the lens of our firefighter example.

Through intense scenario planning and hard-lived experience, firefighters develop a deep understanding of how fires work. They know what makes them spread and how changing temperatures and different fuel sources influence smoke and potential for backdrafts and explosions. They are trained to determine the best time of day or night to hand off from one team to another without losing ground on a rapidly spreading blaze. There are few individuals or teams who are more time-compressed than firefighters. Yet, despite all of their individual and collective talent and experience—and in spite of all of that time pressure— no firefighter rolls onto the scene, jumps out of the truck and immediately starts fighting the fire.

Even with lives and property on the line, first responders and others who work in high-threat environments know that they need to ground themselves and gain an understanding of the situation before deciding how best to respond. They know that each scene has nuances that inform how best to approach the emergency. They are trained to know that their bodies and minds are operating in high alert and recognize that they need to draw on a balance of confidence in their own abilities and the humility to understand that, while they *know* about fire, they do not know the particulars about this fire. A gas fire is not the same as a forest fire which is not the same as an oil fire. Every scene is different, so learning to stop and assess the contours of an emerging situation is fundamental to an effective response to a fire emergency.

While not every What Now? Moment is a house on fire, there is a lot we can learn from emergency responders about dealing with change and uncertain transitions. Each one is different, so learning to stop and assess the contours of an emerging professional or personal disruption or interruption is fundamental to an effective response. We need to consider a combination of expertise and prior understanding and ground it in the humility to accept that our experience and expertise may be more or less relevant to inform our actions in the new environment. Getting there requires us to bust a few myths about change that are repeated so often that it's easy to believe they are true.

Change Myth #1: Change and uncertainty are scary

From the moment you open your eyes in the morning until the moment you close them again at night you are constantly changing and adapting to uncertain situations. The vast majority of those changes come so easily that you don't even register them in your conscious mind. The changes and transitions that register as scary are the ones we perceive as a threat to ourselves or others, which means it's the threat, not the change that prompts fear and discomfort.

Change Myth #2: Some changes are good, and others are bad

We all react differently to change, depending upon who we are and the context in which we find ourselves. A change that one person might perceive to be threatening is someone else's adventure. While we might be more vulnerable to viewing certain kinds of changes as difficult or threatening, to characterize change as good or bad outside of its context can be unhelpful and limiting.

Change Myth #3: I can't deal with uncertainty, so I'm not good at change

If you have stepped into a car, onto a bus or crossed a street, you have proved you can deal with uncertainty and change. Human beings are built for change and adaptation. We are born for it and spend our lives doing it. Learning to apply those fundamental skills to other situations—even threatening ones—is possible with attention, resources, and practice. There is no "normal" when it comes to our response to change, and everyone can get better at navigating it.

These myths point to the critical role that context plays in our perception of change and whether or not we view it as a threat. Let's use that time I got fired (kinda) as an example.

That time I got fired (kinda)

At first blush, getting fired might seem like the type of What Now? Moment that anyone would dread. It taps into fear of losing security and can call into question who we are, what is possible and where we go from here. I came about as close as one could come to experiencing it in the mid-1990s while working for a small, but growing, software startup. I'd taken the position as an attempt to move from the highly regulated and structured electric utility industry into what was then a rapidly emerging tech sector. The position involved supporting the CEO and COO with communications strategy, media relations and crisis planning. A perfect fit given my most recent experience. Or so it seemed.

It became abundantly clear within days of taking the job that the position the company had hired for was not the one they needed to fill. The goals and objectives I was tasked with required fundamentally different skills and experience than we'd discussed during the interview process. I did what I could to adapt, but the gap between their expectations and my experience was too wide to close at the pace required for me to succeed in the position. It only took a few weeks for me to see the handwriting on the wall.

The market for people with my skills was strong at the time, especially among startups, but leaving a job after less than two months was still frowned upon in my industry. To add another layer of stress to the mix, my husband had recently launched a small business that was just starting to gather some steam. That meant my income and benefits were critical to keeping our family of five afloat. This was my What Now? Moment—and, as you might imagine, incendiary emotions were running high.

Follow your dispassion

In a world where following our passion is touted as a useful navigation tool for professional growth and personal fulfillment, I'll admit that the concept of dispassion can seem out of place. Let me be clear, I'm not advocating against finding inspiration and motivation in passion, which is defined in the Oxford English dictionary simply as a strong and barely controllable emotion. In fact, incendiary emotional responses—both positive and negative—can prompt us to pay attention and stay motivated when we need inspiration (more on this in Chapter 10). That said, making sense of our passionate responses at the point of impact of a What Now? Moment can get tricky, especially when we're unsure what's next. So, while following our passion can provide wind at our backs when the way forward is clear, it can also be unhelpful when it creates emotional noise that clouds our judgment or leads us astray when we face uncertain transitions.

In the case of my What Now? Moment, putting my incendiary emotions aside briefly allowed me to take some initiative and begin looking for a new position, despite the possible fallout that might come my way for leaving quickly. Fortunately, I was able to secure a new position rather quickly with an online learning company. I remember sitting at my desk in the warehouse of a not-so-sexy open office, breathing a sigh of relief when I received the news. I had planned to give my two weeks' notice on my way out at the end of the day, when the COO came by my office to tell me they were giving me two weeks to get my house in order, but they had to let me go.

A month earlier, that same conversation would have sent me into a tailspin. I can just imagine how it would have felt to have a two-week clock ticking on a salary and benefits that were critical to keeping the lights on for me and my family. Not only that, but I'm also sure that the misstep would have led me to question my decision to leave a more stable industry for a burgeoning one, and that I may have come to doubt my suitability for work in the emerging tech sector. Undoubtedly, my threat response would have engaged—and a call home may have prompted the same for my husband, Martin. Instead, because I had faxed (yes, faxed) my signed contract to my new employer earlier that day, the same news held no threat. Same scenario, different perspective, different response.

This example raises some interesting questions about how we can prepare for What Now? Moments and equip ourselves to better navigate uncertain transitions that feel threatening. In my case, preparing for what felt like (and eventually proved to be) an inevitable parting of ways, allowed me to find a new way forward before the spark of a threat became an inferno. As a result, I was able to reorient myself within the space between What Now? and what comes next in a way that both served my needs and made space in the organization for someone who was a better fit. On both sides of the equation—mine and my employers'—this anecdote illustrates a helpful practice I call *active resilience*.

Building active resilience

When most people hear the word resilience, they think about emotional resilience and what it takes to "bounce back" from adversity. More recently, the concept has been expanded to include concepts such as post-traumatic growth and anti-fragility (Taleb, 2014) that suggest we can do more than bounce back when we face a disruption; we can actually be better for it (see Appendix B for resources). My exploration of stuckness led me to the question of how, like emergency services professionals, we might prepare ourselves to be resilient before we encounter adversity rather than hoping to bounce back after the fact. At the time I was particularly interested in how we design services for transformation and wellbeing and what resources people need to keep from getting stuck in the face of uncertainty and change. That's when I first encountered the work of Dr Michael Ungar and his robust view of resilience.

Michael Ungar is the principal investigator for the Resilience Research Centre at Dalhousie University in Halifax, Canada, where he is a professor in the school of social work. His research and practice in the fields of social and psychological resilience spans decades, continents and contexts—from children to adults to organizations and communities. He defines resilience in adversity as "both the capacity of individuals to navigate their way to the psychological, social, cultural, and physical resources that sustain their wellbeing, and their capacity individually and collectively to negotiate for these resources to be provided in culturally meaningful ways" (Ungar, 2019). What I love about Ungar's view of resilience is the emphasis on resource gathering, community building and the cultural context in which these elements come together. This points to the value of developing a practice of "active resilience" that we can pursue—individually, communally, and organizationally—before, during and after we face What Now? Moments.

Ungar's definition focuses less on resilience as a trait or the passive act of waiting to "bounce back," and more on the agency that we have to pursue resources (or to seek assistance finding them). As a result, we have something to focus on when we don't know what to do. This simple act of having agency, which refers to having some control over the circumstance in which we find ourselves when we feel like we have none, can help us to temper our initial reaction to threat and engage in *dispassionate curiosity*, directed toward identifying the resources we have, the resources we need and how we might connect with them. This helps us to focus more on what might be possible in the face of uncertainty rather than ruminate on incendiary emotions and fear of what may go wrong. It also offers a powerful way to support others who are facing What Now? Moments by pointing them in the direction of identifying and gathering the resources they need rather than offering uniform and overly simplistic advice.

But where do we begin? Identifying where we are more or less vulnerable to perceive change as a threat can be a very helpful starting point for understanding what kinds of resources to gather before we encounter a disruption. This helps us to be as prepared as we can be when a What Now? Moment pushes those buttons.

Identifying where we are more or less vulnerable to perceive change as a threat can be a very helpful starting point for understanding what kinds of resources to gather before we encounter a disruption.

Equipping for active resilience

If you're like most of the people I encounter in this work, you've already begun the process of connecting with emotional, material, physical and social resources through professional and personal development practices like coaching, psychotherapy, exercise, meditation, and mindfulness practices, playing games, socializing with friends, interacting with family, and connecting with community resources. Whether it's filled to the brim or has just one or two items in it, this is the active resilience toolbox you're starting with today. As I share some new tools and tactics with you in the coming pages and chapters, I encourage you to use them to complement what is already working and help you to connect with relevant resources when emotions are running high. Rather than advocate for a new way of addressing change, I'm encouraging you to stick with what works, supplement where necessary, and practice using the tools you already have in ways that will make you better equipped to face What Now? Moments now and in the future. I'm also encouraging you to clarify where you are more or less resourced psychologically, socially, culturally, or physically when you encounter What Now? Moments so you can begin to think about how you might access relevant resources before, during and after you're feeling lost in transition.

The resilience wheel

Recognizing where we are more or less likely to be resilient can help us to be better prepared the next time a What Now? Moment throws a potentially distracting spark on our emotions. The resilience wheel in Figure 2.1 provides a fast (and fun) way

FIGURE 2.1 Resilience wheel

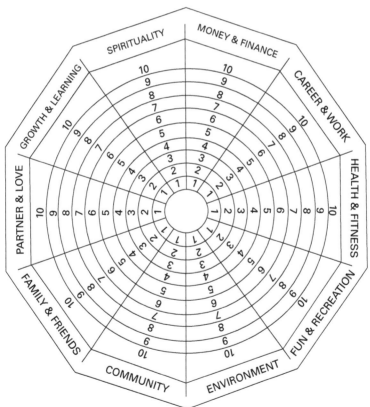

to think about our perceived resilience across some common domains. Here's how it works. Start by grabbing two different-colored pens, because you'll complete two self-assessments on the same wheel. You can do the exercise right here in the book, or visit my website and print a free pdf.

Choose one of your colored pens and rate yourself on a scale of 1 (least resilient) to 10 (most resilient) if you encountered a *huge disruption* in each of these 10 domains. I'll give you an example from my own experience to illustrate. I love my work and value my position teaching at St. John's University in New York. I would be very disappointed if something happened, and I could no longer serve there. That said, I have a rather high risk tolerance when it comes to finances. I've had times in my life that I lived on very little and others where I had more than I needed. Yes, I am a college professor, a writer, and a consultant—but I've also supported myself waiting tables and cleaning other people's houses. Since I am willing to do either kind of work to keep me afloat financially, I feel confident that I would navigate to the resources I need if I had a huge disruption and needed to adjust to pay the bills. Given that, I might place a line on the number 9 or 10 in the money and finance space in the wheel or in the career and work category to represent a high self-perception of resilience in this area.

When it comes to family and friends, it's a different story. Close human interactions are not my strong suit, and I can be very hurt when they go wrong. That makes me more vulnerable to a threat response in that area, so I might fill in the 4 or 5 for that category. Taking each category on the resilience wheel one by one (alone, with a group or with a professional), you can identify your unique spectrum of potential strengths and weaknesses when you encounter What Now? Moments. The completed wheel will look something like what you see in Figure 2.2.

Once you've completed the wheel with a huge disruption in mind, complete it again on the same wheel with a different-colored pen. This time, rather than focus on a major disruption, think about how you might respond to a *daily interruption*.

FIGURE 2.2   Resilience wheel

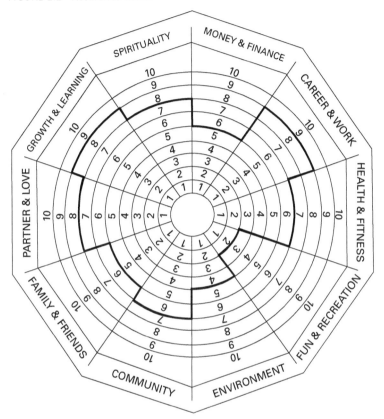

Nothing catastrophic. Just the day-to-day issues of annoying co-workers, meetings that go over schedule and other minor frustrations that get under our skin. Since we often see threat differently in the same domain when the stakes change, your final wheel might look something like Figure 2.3.

Once you've completed both self-assessments on the resilience wheel, you'll have a deeper insight into where you have ample resources to respond to What Now? Moments and where you might want to identify the resources you might need to prepare in the event that you face pressure in one or more of these domains.

FIGURE 2.3 Resilience wheel

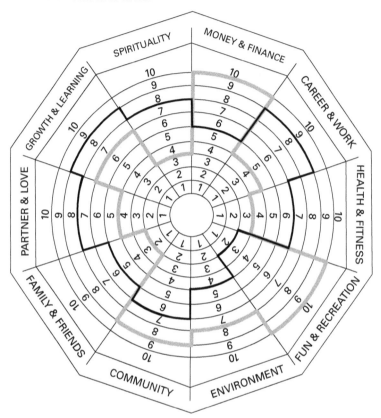

You can use this tool in a variety of ways to reflect on your overall resilience or in different contexts and at different scales. Some people choose to layer their self-assessment across life domains (i.e. at work, at home, on a team, etc.). Doing so can help you to get a better sense of how you might be likely to respond when the stakes are high and if that is different to how you might respond when the stakes are low.

Using my example above, I might be quite resilient if I had a catastrophic financial setback—but when I forget my phone and wallet on the way to work and don't have money to buy coffee and lunch, that type of a minor annoyance can get under my skin. If you are unsure or wonder about how you come across to others, you can even ask your partner, your therapist, or a trusted friend to share their observations about times they've seen you face What Now? Moments and whether they see places where you tend to be actively resilient and places where you might need more resources. At work, you can run this exercise with a group or team to see where the team is or is not resilient as a means to identify places where resources are needed.

It's important to note that this is not a contest—nor is the goal to be a 10 across the board. Despite how we often talk about resilience, no one is resilient in all things or lacking resilience in all things. Resilience is not a binary all or nothing. Instead, it is about recognizing that we are all resilient in some areas of our life and less resilient in others.

Overall, we can take steps to become more resilient through an engaged practice to focus on a specific domain of our wheel and choose to gather resources to better equip ourselves in that area. The point is to use the wheel to shine a light on places where you might view change or transition as a threat. This can help you to avoid the fear loop and access the curiosity loop when change inevitably comes your way. Once you become more familiar with your perceived vulnerabilities with respect to resilience, you might have a better sense of what types of situations might require you to gather extra resources when under pressure—not as a matter of weakness or failure, but as a way to have what you need in your metaphorical backpack to make your way through uncharted territory. It can also provide a way to make sense of the information you've gathered in all of the books, resources, courses, and professional/personal development materials you've engaged with over the years!

It's important to recognize that, like responding to What Now? Moments, practicing dispassionate curiosity and building active resilience are very context- and resource-dependent endeavors. We all start in different places and under different constraints. Practicing active resilience involves a commitment to humbly accept that, regardless of our background, training, or experience, gathering resources for our professional and personal journeys is a lifelong practice that each of us will approach in our own way—individually, in community, and in and outside of the institutions where we work and engage with the world.

As we learn to engage uncertain transitions more like emergency services professionals, with confidence and humility, we can then develop practices and approaches to help us to gather the resources and fundamental skills we need to thrive in uncertain times. This invites us to accept that we are all equally subject to the threat response, and that there is value in learning to, as Ungar suggests, navigate to the resources we need in ways that are culturally and contextually relevant to us.

For some, this might mean developing a mindfulness practice. For others, that might feel out of reach. For some, it will be faith or spirituality. For others, that may feel abstract or off-putting. Some will dance or sing or engage with the arts. Others will use exercise or community or therapy or an executive coach as resources for active resilience. I am agnostic about your approach to this. I only advocate that you consider the benefits to you and those you serve if you develop your own methods and approaches to make space for you or your team to face your next What Now? Moment with dispassionate curiosity and active resilience rather than fear and trepidation. Of course, that's not easy if we're constantly expected to move fast and pivot.

TAKEAWAYS

- Learning to stop during *What Now?* Moments can be easier said than done—especially when change feels like a threat.

- Shifting from incendiary reaction to a dispassionate and curious response can transform our relationship with change.

- Practicing active resilience can help us to gather the resources we need to gain stability as we navigate uncertain transitions.

CHAPTER THREE

Don't pivot

Active waiting and minding our metaphors

"How do I know whether or not I should pivot?" I couldn't help but smile to myself as this question was posed by a breakout author under contract for two books (while promoting a third!). The earnest question came during one of my weekly public conversations about the philosophy and practice of finding our way when the way isn't clear. "The issue is that I am a person with interdisciplinary interests who is not much of a multitasker," she continued, "and I'm not sure if I should integrate, remove things from my plate or..." Like so many others who find themselves on the threshold of uncharted territory, her voice trailed off toward an elusive choice she was not yet able to articulate.

I knew from previous conversations that the stumbling block was about more than an incapacity to multitask. Like so many of us who are living complex lives that span multiple domains, making sense of competing professional and personal pressures and commitments requires something more than a quick choice.

"Whether or not to pivot is a concrete decision," I told her. "It sounds like you're not there yet."

Pivot, persevere... or inquire?

The pivot metaphor became popular in Silicon Valley startup circles in the early to mid-2000s with the release of several books about entrepreneurship. One of the most popular among them, *The Lean Startup* by Eric Ries, outlines an approach to innovation designed to bring new products and services to market as quickly as possible, in a very systematic way (Ries, 2011). The idea is simple... and effective. Learn what works (or what doesn't) by getting new products into the hands of customers as quickly as possible. Ries's "build, measure, learn" framework has proved to be an effective way to use customer feedback to determine whether to change strategic and tactical direction (pivot) or remain on the current course (persevere). This systematic approach to building fast while mitigating risk has been the darling of startup founders and venture investors, so it's no surprise that many people have embraced the pivot metaphor in other contexts. I hear it now in conversations with students who are thinking about changing majors, individuals thinking about a career change, and in conversations about the future of work, education and learning.

So, what's my problem with a pivot?

Let me start by saying that the pivot has its place. When we stand at a turning point and the choices we face are distinct, viewing next steps through the lens of a pivot metaphor may keep us from getting lost or stalled in indecision and inspire us to act (see Chapter 10 for more on this). But, when we face What Now? Moments, the binary choice to either pivot or persevere can force a decision before we have time to gather resources and orient ourselves in what is effectively new terrain.

Author and psychiatrist Owen Muir, M.D. said it best when we discussed my hesitation about the pivot metaphor. "The pivot makes sense if you're a VC-backed startup trying to find a better product-market fit," he told me. "Finding a better self-world fit is much harder to do." I thought long and hard about the notion of a self-world fit after that conversation, and how important this distinction between what works for a business and what works for people finding their way in the world is when we consider adopting business principles like pivoting to guide our thinking about the human aspects of navigating uncertainty and change.

The binary choice to either pivot or persevere can force a decision before we have time to gather resources and orient ourselves in what is effectively new terrain.

What's a pivot anyway?

In its most simple definition, to pivot is to turn or rotate around a point. Many examples apply, like a hinge on a door or a player's foot on the basketball court. The pressure we feel (real or perceived) to move through uncertain transitions faster than is truly necessary can sometimes make us feel like that basketball player, stuck with one foot in place, turning around in circles hoping to find an open route to make a pass or take a shot. That's why when the author at the opening of this chapter—or anyone else who is facing an uncertain transition at work or at home—asks, "How do you know when to pivot?" I remind them that, despite the accelerating pace of business and life, most What Now? Moments don't require us to pivot. We get to lift our foot off the ground, put the basketball down and create our own, less limiting metaphors to guide our thinking about where we are, where we're going in the space between What Now? and what comes next.

Metaphors (and why they matter)

When we think of metaphors (if we think of metaphors at all!) it tends to be as a vehicle for telling a good story. We know we can bring a pitch, a speech, or a written communication to life by describing a goal as a *mountain to climb*, a challenge as *a river to cross,* or a competitor as an *enemy to vanquish*. When issues run deep we see the *tip of the iceberg*. Our vision for the future sits *on the horizon* and, as we've discussed, a change of direction is *a pivot*. But there is more to metaphor than good storytelling. Whether or not we are aware of it, the way we use metaphor shapes our perceptions of the world and how we operate in it (Lakoff, 2006).

Let's take the way we think about the human brain as an example.

We know exactly what someone means when they say that a particular way of thinking, being or doing is "not how I'm wired." But what are the implications of thinking about being or not being "wired" to do something? Conceptually, "wired" is rooted in a metaphor that casts humans as a computer or other electronic device. In this view, we are "wired" to do things or think things or be a particular way. We may or may not be able to be "rewired" to do things or think things or be a different way. How does this framing influence the way we approach learning? Motivation? Identity? Ability? If I'm not wired for something, why would I apply myself to pursue it? Why would I rely on you to collaborate with me on something that requires it? What does it mean about how I learn? How I interact with others? How I navigate uncertainty?

Let's play with this idea for a bit.

Since we are moving rapidly toward an increasingly wireless world, it is interesting to think about how we might view being "wired" 100 years from now. A time when plugging something into a wall or weaving hundreds and thousands of wires together to connect things will seem quaint, old-fashioned and remarkably static. Brain *plasticity* already provides a more dynamic metaphor for how the brain develops and changes over time, which is arguably more inspiring from a learning perspective. And who knows what metaphors we will use in the future to make the abstract notion of how our brains work more concrete? The point here is that humans use metaphors to make sense of the world around us—and the ones we choose can both help and hinder the way we approach change.

> QUESTION FOR REFLECTION
>
> What are some metaphors you use to think about transitions and change?

There is a rich and diverse stream of research focused on understanding how metaphor shapes and influences human thought and action (see Appendix C). Authors Lakoff and Johnson, for instance, have devoted much of their professional lives to exploring how humans engage with metaphor. Their ground-breaking research on the topic suggests that our use of conceptual metaphor to think and communicate is fundamental to how we make sense of the world in a way that is unavoidable and mostly unconscious (Lakoff and Johnson, 1980). Harvard Business School professor and metaphor elicitation expert Gerald Zaltman made the same observation in his work with tens of thousands of people using his patented metaphor elicitation technique, ZMET™ (Zaltman, 2008). According to Zaltman and his colleagues, deep metaphors exist across cultures and "capture what anthropologists, psychologists, and sociologists call human universals, or near universals, the traits and behaviors found in nearly all societies."

Zaltman and his colleagues describe seven deep metaphors (balance, transformation, journey, container, connection, resource, and control). While every one of these universal metaphor types can be useful for understanding our thoughts and actions when we face uncertain transitions, journey and container metaphors can be especially helpful when we think about alternatives to the pivot metaphor and contemplate the potential benefits of opening up space for inquiry and exploration when the way forward is unclear.

Opening space for active waiting

Carving out space and time to make sense of changing circumstances before choosing how best to move forward is neither a luxury nor a waste of time—it is a necessity. Even when time is short, moving away from the "foot on the court" basketball mentality to opening up dedicated space and time to acclimate to new circumstances can help reduce the sense of urgency (and threat) we feel when we face a What Now? Moment. This is not about creating space to sit on your hands or getting lost in analysis. It is about developing a practice of pausing our journey to create space for what I call active waiting. Active waiting is the intentional process of creating time and space to gather resources, reorient to new surroundings and engage in inquiry and exploration when faced with uncertain transitions.

A mountain climbing metaphor provides a useful way to think about this.

Climbing Mt. Everest or another of the world's largest mountains is not a straight shot to the summit. Climbers move from periods of trekking to time spent in base camps as they make their way up the mountain. Trekking to base camp requires certain skills, capacities, resources, and approaches. The journey may be difficult, but the direction and intention are clear. The climber has a clear goal and knows where they are headed.

Trekking to base camp is a helpful metaphor for thinking about how we execute on a clear goal. We know where we are, we know where we are going, we gather the resources we need and make the trek. We may hit barriers to progress, but the objective is clear until we reach our goal or encounter a What Now? Moment along the way.

Active waiting is the intentional process of creating time and space to gather resources, reorient to new surroundings and engage in inquiry and exploration when faced with uncertain transitions.

Once a climber reaches base camp, there is a pause in the *journey* up the mountain. Activities and objectives change from pressing forward to reflecting on the trek and equipping for the next legs of the climb. Base camp provides a *container* within the larger journey that is about much more than stopping to take a rest. In stark contrast to Reis's quick pivot, climbers and their teams spend an average of one to two months at Everest base camp. Days in base camp are spent focusing on what they and their teams need to replenish, reorient and reacclimate to be sure climbers are physically and mentally prepared to reach the summit. This period of *active waiting* requires different skills, capacities and resources than are necessary for the trek to base camp or the climb to the summit. While not focused on pressing forward, activities in the container of base camp are as important as what takes place on the journey to the summit. Leaving base camp too soon or without the resources the climbers and their teams need can have deadly consequences. So, to spend time in the nurturing, exploratory space of the base camp before returning to the climb increases the likelihood of reaching the summit safely.

The successful climber recognizes both the value of the trek and the time of recalibration and replenishment at base camp— the journey and the container. As a result, they are practiced and adept at moving between them (or working under the advice

FIGURE 3.1 Base camp

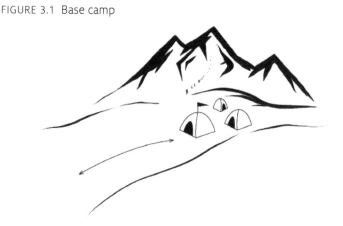

and support of someone who does!). This mountain climbing metaphor not only provides a useful illustration of the process of moving from execution to exploration on a project or endeavor, but it is also a wonderful example of why metaphor is such a powerful tool for making sense of What Now? Moments. Too often we favor execution over exploration, when both are critical parts of any journey. As a result, we press (or pivot) through uncertain transitions rather than making time to recalibrate, reorient and tease out new possibilities that emerge when our plans are disrupted or interrupted. By consciously shifting from execution to exploration—from the trek to basecamp—we get the best of ourselves and our teams in both domains.

Time horizons and active waiting

When we open up space for active waiting, it is helpful to consider the time horizon we're operating on and ask ourselves if it is real or perceived. A *time horizon* is *a point in the future that is determined to measure or complete a task*. It can be as precise as a fixed deadline, or as loose as a date on the calendar to reflect on your chosen trajectory. In any case, how we think about time horizons influences our expectations and the pace at which we work and live. When a person decides that they need to build a successful business by the time they're 30, for instance, they are setting a time horizon that will guide their steps through their 20s. When we (or people in our lives) set expectations that we should be married or have children at a certain age or before or after we reach a career milestone, we are setting out time horizons. Some time horizons are fixed—you can't win a 30 under 30 award when you are 45. Others have the potential to be fluid, whether or not we perceive them to be. Creating time for active waiting at points of transition provides us with an opportunity to pause and discover just how flexible our time horizons can be.

Metaphors and the What Now? Moment

While the mountain climbing metaphor is useful to think about creating time and space for active waiting, there is no single metaphor or framework that encapsulates all that goes into finding our way when the way isn't clear. Sure, the mountain encapsulates the resource gathering, direction finding and movement toward an aspiration or goal that some people find inspiring. But it might not land for someone who has a multitude of interests and is not setting out on a singular quest to reach a particular goal. For them a metaphor of exploring a galaxy or planting a garden might be more resonant.

And that's just fine.

Our focus on metaphor is not about choosing a single way to think about uncertain transitions and learning to adapt to it. Instead, understanding the metaphors that guide our thinking is about acknowledging that people naturally make sense of the world in terms of metaphors, and that understanding that the ones we rely upon can be helpful (or unhelpful) when we consider them in practice. Let's ground this with a few examples.

Metaphors in practice

My research into stuckness and what it takes to navigate uncertain transitions sparked a What Now? Moment for me. I'd made a shift from a 17-year professional communications career into academia in the early 2000s, and the transition from viewing myself as a communications professional to a university professor was clear and unambiguous. There were some detours and surprises along the way, but from an identity perspective, it was a textbook pivot. That changed when my research expanded into professional engagements with individual leaders, teams, and organizations. People close to me knew I was primarily an educator, but bringing my work into the field meant others began referring to me as a coach, a consultant, or a facilitator. On the face of it, none of these roles fit my work—especially when viewed outside of a job description with a metaphor lens. My approach to professional and personal development did not fit the way a coach works. Consulting came closer, and it suggested an expertise dynamic that I could have sold if I cared to, but did not describe the way I engage with my clients and research participants—especially since my work transcends commerce and is applied at school, with individuals, with teams, etc. I decided to contemplate my own metaphors and concluded that neither coach nor consultant made sense for me. Facilitator came even closer, but still lacked the depth and breadth of my engagements. As I continued to consider possible ways to think about how I worked, I expanded my inquiry to consider how people outside of my field approached their work. Doing so led me to a surprising, but apt metaphor. I approach my work like a midwife.

Midwives have expertise, but they don't call the shots. They engage with expectant mothers as equals, acknowledging that they are there to support based upon the needs, desires and unique circumstances of the expectant mother and their family. They recognize that all pregnancies are different—from the resource perspective, the social perspective and the manner in which people want to make their own choices about how, where and with whom they want to approach the birth experience. They adapt themselves to particular rituals, traditions, and cultures where they engage. And, perhaps most importantly, they recognize that they are partners in bringing the baby to life—not in raising it!

Once I saw myself in this way it became much easier for me to organize my work in a way that makes sense to me. It also helped me to shake some unhelpful expectations that came with some other ways of framing my work. People I work with still like to think of me as a coach, a consultant, a facilitator, or an educator—and that's fine by me. The midwife metaphor is an organizing principle that helps me to understand my place in a world, not a communication or marketing tool (although I nod to it with the name of my company, WOMBLab). Considering my work in this way helped me to see the power of intentionally using metaphor to orient myself in times of uncertainty and was instrumental in my exploration of its use as a tool to help others to make sense of their uncertain transitions.

I worked with a building contractor, as an example, who decided to go to college in his 40s to explore new career options. He was committed to the process and more than willing to do the schoolwork, but battled self-doubt and anxiety with regard to his ability to complete the program and actually make something out of it. I asked him to tell me more about what he was going through, but he wasn't able to articulate an answer beyond saying that he was skeptical about his capacity to make a successful transition to a new career upon graduation. I gave him a brief overview of conceptual metaphors and how they shape our view of the world, and asked him to share his situation, placing himself as a character in a movie. Without hesitation, he described a scene in detail. "You know those huge ships, the freighters with curved sides that are four or five stories above the ocean?" he asked. "Well," he continued. "I'm the guy who jumped off the side of the boat who's stranded in the ocean with no way to get back in. Graduation and a new job are beyond the horizon that I can't see—or maybe they're not there at all." We sat quietly for a moment while he reflected on the metaphor. Eventually he started to laugh, and I joined him when he said, "and I barely know how to swim!" No wonder he was feeling stressed!

In the space of less than an hour we were able to come up with several new possible transition narratives grounded in less threatening metaphors. Although he still had his fears and concerns about what was ahead of him, he described the process of reframing the uncharted territory between where he was and an unknown future as a relief and continued to use both the old metaphor and the new ones to gauge his thoughts and actions in the weeks and months that followed. He told me later that, whenever he found himself stressed out about school or stuck in transition, he thought about himself flailing in the middle of the ocean and started laughing.

The beauty of exploring the use of metaphor as a tool for understanding is that it can be used in team and client environments as well. In an online conversation with a group of people who were new to the concept of using metaphor in this way, I asked for an example from participants. A woman who was having some challenges with workflow, communication and interaction with a new client volunteered to share her challenge and frustratedly described her interaction with the team as "too many cooks in the kitchen." Rather than rely on me to help her to come up with an alternative, other participants in the session, all of whom were new to using metaphors in this way, chimed in with wonderful ideas about alternate ways this individual might view the situation as she prepared for a meeting with the client scheduled for later that day. Together, this group of mostly strangers considered what might happen if the individual were to shift from viewing the members of the team as "cooks in the kitchen" to "a variety of ingredients" that, when combined together in the right order, right measure and right timing, could create a delicious recipe. She took both metaphors to the meeting that afternoon and used them as the stepping-off point for what she had feared might be a contentious encounter with her client. Instead, she later told me, the metaphors paved the way for some clarifying conversations that not only got things unstuck in the moment but provided a useful language for the future.

Rebecca Taylor, a world-renowned strategist and consultant for museums, galleries, art fairs and luxury brands found value in exploring metaphor when her world was disrupted in a positive way. New opportunities in an adjacent field opened surprising and unexpected doors that expanded her influence and placed her in the spotlight, a role she valued for her clients, but not for herself. After she shared this sentiment in an online session about the use of metaphor for wayfinding, another participant reached out and offered an alternative view: to step into the sunshine, not the spotlight. "I'm writing that down," she told him. "It resonates so much because I love the sunshine but loathe the spotlight. One is full of joy and warmth, the other ego, so the framing is really poignant for me."

As you can see from these examples and the many others I draw upon to discuss change in this book, What Now? Moments may present as a river to be crossed, a garden to be planted and tended to, a switching yard, the space between conception and birth, and so many others. There are countless metaphors we can use to make sense of uncertain transitions and the challenges and opportunities they provide for us. This means that we can choose to create personal metaphors to guide sensemaking in our day-to-day lives and can play with metaphor as a tool to help make sense of how we navigate in the world.

We can choose to create personal metaphors to guide sensemaking in our day-to-day lives and can play with metaphor as a tool to make sense of how we navigate in the world.

This can involve developing a practice of observing how we use metaphor in thought and action and intentionally adapting and shifting metaphors in context as a way to understand how we view change. Here are some prompts if you'd like to try it out. Keep in mind that, as mentioned previously, the goal of this exercise is not to find the perfect metaphor. Instead, it is to get a deeper understanding of how metaphor is already guiding our thoughts and how we might become more aware of where metaphor helps and hinders our approach to What Now? Moments.

EXERCISE Playing with metaphor

Spend one day observing how you and those around you use metaphor—especially in the context of change, transition, and uncertainty. You may choose to focus on work or home or online. Collect as many metaphors as you can and observe how they help or hinder understanding and communication.

• Which metaphors resonate with you?

• Which metaphors create barriers to understanding?

• What is the most helpful change metaphor you observed?

• How might you use it to guide your thinking in the future?

• What is the least helpful change metaphor you observed?

• How might you use it to guide your thinking in the future?

Identifying your own metaphors is useful to get a conscious and unconscious sense of where we are when we're feeling lost or unmoored. When working in groups, the process of comparing and contrasting where metaphors align or clash can help to capture unspoken similarities and differences among group members and get a deeper understanding of where barriers to progress and misunderstandings might arise. In either case, I often ask participants to draw pictures, make collages, play with LEGO—anything that helps them to surface the metaphors they use—consciously and unconsciously—to make sense of change and points of intersection.

As you continue to play with your own change metaphors you will see that even the most helpful metaphor breaks down in some contexts. That is fine. We learn as much from where a metaphor fails as where it works. If you have to convince yourself or your team too that MY metaphor is the correct one for YOUR circumstance, then the metaphor you're using is unhelpful. The goal is not to identify a single perfect metaphor and adapt ourselves to its use. Instead, we hope to identify multiple—maybe even mixed—metaphors as a tool to understand where we are and where we hope to go from here.

So, if climbing the corporate ladder or finding your "true north" is helpful—stick with that and use it as a tool to guide you on your journey. If those metaphors cause confusion or leave you feeling stuck, then consider others. All in all, I'm not interested in advocating a single new, "better" metaphor to describe how we approach our competing professional and personal commitments in the new terrain of work in the 2020s and beyond. Instead, I invite you to add metaphor to your sense-making toolbox, so you are better equipped when What Now? Moments leave you feeling lost or disoriented.

TAKEAWAYS

- Business concepts like the pivot can be helpful to guide strategy and growth in tech companies but are less helpful when we face What Now? Moments in other contexts.

- Making time and space for *active waiting* allows us to pause our journey and create a container for inquiry and exploration when we face uncertain transitions.

- Reconsidering the metaphors that guide our thoughts and actions can help us to reframe our thinking and reduce perceptions of threat.

CHAPTER FOUR

Lost in transition

Creating learning space to get your bearings

"I don't want to pick a lane." Erica wasn't the first person to say that to me, but she is certainly one of the most remarkable. She's a CEO and founder of Langston League, a published novelist, and an educator and former school administrator whose Cardi B cover-turned-geography lesson went viral online and in television and print media. Not entirely surprising, since Erica was a rapper and HBO Def Poet in her teens. Now she is expanding into educational entertainment, television writing and has other high-profile projects on the near horizon.

Oh, and she is only 33.

When we first connected, Erica was trying to make sense of her varied expertise and wrestling with the advice she'd received countless times. "You're doing too much," her mentors, teachers, family and leadership experts told her, "You need to pick a lane." As the gig economy mindset spills over into even the most traditional career paths, more and more people find themselves challenging 20th-century paradigms and engaging in a constellation of activities rather than a singular career goal or focus. Unfortunately, our systems and even our greatest supporters haven't all gotten the memo.

It was clear to Erica that her confidants had her best interests in mind. She *was* burning the candle at more than both ends, and she *did* need to pace herself. But she had a deep sense that doubling down on just one of her many talents was not the only way to sustain herself and bring her aspirations to life. Despite her ongoing successes, she felt exhausted, overwhelmed and unclear about how to reconcile her commitment to her work while maintaining her own health and wellbeing in the face of competing priorities and limited resources. She perceived herself to be at the junction of two less than desirable paths forward— to give up some of these thriving initiatives or to continue grinding down her current path and suffer the inevitable burnout. Neither choice felt right. In our conversations and chats she often described herself as feeling both inspired and lost at the prospect of charting a less traditional and focused career and life course. And she is not alone.

Words like lost and disoriented come up frequently in my discussions with people who find themselves on the threshold of uncertainty and change. This may explain why uncertain transitions spark incendiary emotions that throw us into the fear loop. Just the thought of being lost in the woods, the jungle, the desert, or any remote place without a means of finding a way out leaves most people feeling physically and emotionally vulnerable. Being lost causes fear and anxiety, which makes a lot of sense, since losing our sense of direction in the wild can quickly become a matter of life and death.

Remarkably, it doesn't take being in the wilderness to conjure equivalent fear and anxiety of being lost in physical spaces. Learners experience a similar sense of being lost or stuck, sometimes called a disjunction or a disorienting dilemma, when they encounter concepts that cause them to question prior ideas, beliefs and values in ways that challenge their self-concept (see Appendix D). Thus, when people find themselves lost in transition, we encounter a one-two punch. The ill-defined space between What Now? and what comes next taxes both our self-concept (who am I?) *and* our self-direction (where do I go from here?) (Oldham, 2015). Stopping to acknowledge feeling lost and understanding how it affects us is fundamental to reorienting ourselves in uncharted territory.

The psychology of lost

Kenneth Hill, professor emeritus of psychology at St. Mary's University in Halifax, Nova Scotia has been thinking about how people behave when they are lost since the mid-1980s. Professor Hill's interest in the subject was born in tragedy when he joined the search and rescue efforts to find a lost nine-year-old boy who was found deceased nine days after he went missing near his home in Canada. According to Hill, there was no rhyme or reason to the way the search was conducted because, at that time, there was a fundamental lack of understanding of how people think and behave when they are lost in the woods. His pioneering work has since led to a rich and now expansive field of research into the emotional and behavioral ways that people respond to being lost.

According to Hill, being lost involves two simple but distinct components—experiencing disorientation and a lack of an effective means to reorient oneself (Hill, 2011). While his work is focused on the experiences of backwoods travelers, hunters, hikers and others who find themselves lost in the wilderness, the parallels are evident in stories like Erica's. She had many possible paths in front of her but could not see an obvious or effective means of orienting herself in a way that honored her broad talents and varied ambitions. Despite being highly successful in each of several professional and personal domains, she found herself without a clear sense of direction, feeling stuck and unsure how to proceed. Rather than choose, I invited her to stop and create a transitional space for inquiry as a means to consider other possibilities and explore new options.

Creating transitional learning space

Rather than ruminate on feelings of being stuck or unsure, uncertain transitions can be an invitation to ask new questions and explore opportunities we may not have considered *before* we make firm choices or commitments. Think of it as creating an ad hoc personal learning lab. A creative space to develop your practice of active waiting and dispassionate curiosity that is designed by you, for you, and aligned to your needs, context, and resources. Emergency services professionals do this when they create an emergency operations center on the site of an event or at another location. The climbers we discussed earlier have it at base camp. For an individual like Erica, it can be in a journal, on a white board, in the corner of a home office, or coordinated online with software or an app.

If you're working with a team, you can create shared space in the office or in a collaborative space online. None of it needs to be fancy. It can be a fixed spot or created on the fly. The context, time constraints and available resources will guide what's appropriate and possible. All that matters is that it be a space where questions, new ideas and an exploratory mindset are valued and supported. A space where fears and threats are voiced as areas inviting creative attention rather than a reactive response. The point is not to create an extra step in your process, but to intentionally create a third space between where you were before the What Now? Moment and where you will be when you reorient around a new course of action (or recommit to the course you're on). Sometimes called a neutral zone or liminal space in anthropology (Van Gennep, 2019), this transitional learning space is both distinct and ill-defined. It is uncharted territory where we acknowledge that we have more questions than answers. It's the container where we have space to recognize that we are not ready to decide until we make sense of the situation we're in, and take active steps to gain a deeper understanding of what potential routes forward exist outside of our first thoughts (and our comfort zones).

It is important to note here that creating a transitional learning space is not about finding the answer. It is about accepting that there is rarely a single right or wrong answer in the wake of a What Now? Moment. That's what makes them so difficult. Choosing between A and B is much easier than making sense of abundant possibilities in a world where there is no single route to building a successful company or career and living a good life. So, if you've embraced the call to stop and are eager to move on to the part of the book that offers immediate solutions or quick fixes, you picked up the wrong book. Instead, now that we've begun to settle the threat response and gather resources (active resilience), pause (active waiting), and commit to a process of reflection, inquiry and learning, we're ready to think about learning in the liminal space between What Now? and what comes next.

Learning in liminal space

Liminal learning involves creating a container for creative problem solving where learners intentionally reorient themselves around new information and possibilities in times of uncertainty and change. According to education expert Maggie Savin-Baden, that can lead to a "shift in identity or role perception, so that issues and concerns are seen and heard in new and different ways" (Savin-Baden, 2008). So, the very shift of identity and self-concept that sparks our incendiary emotions and throws us into a threat response is just what we need to tap into new ideas and consider alternative possibilities. This is what makes learning in the liminal so exciting—and so terrifying! This may seem obvious, but identity shifts are no small matter when it comes to our sense of who we are, where we are, and where we are going.

Whether we are in professional or personal settings, changes to our work or life status can lead to deeper, meaningful questions like: Who will I be if I make this change? What will I have to sacrifice? Will my reputation take a hit if I fail? This can raise the stakes of what can appear to be a minor change—like moving to a new team—and elevate our perception of the potential consequences if things don't go as expected. As a result, transitions and change are about more than simply accepting new ideas, approaches or circumstances, as many leaders mistakenly believe. Instead, organizational changes and work and life transitions outside of organizations can challenge identities and shift personal and professional trajectories in ways that lead to deep, existential questions about who we are and where we're meant to be. Until we settle these questions, the threat to identity and self-direction can lead to avoidance, push back, or unwarranted certainty that can create barriers to progress as we approach the task of finding our way when we feel lost or displaced. That's why developing practices that help us to get our bearings when we face interruptions and disruptions is so important.

Getting our bearings: the myth of true north

When Erica's loved ones encouraged her to pick a lane they were working on a common and well-worn 20th-century paradigm: the way to get ahead in life is to set goals and focus all of your attention, resources and time on bringing them to life. In that view, What Now? Moments and uncertain transitions simply become bumps on the road that may cause angst or require a detour, but the objective remains clear. Become a doctor, lawyer, firefighter or small business owner. Get married. Have children. Participate in the life of your community. In this paradigm we approach work and life as many people would a cross-country drive. Pick a destination. Map out a route to get there. Even if you take the scenic route, the destination is clear—even if the particulars are not.

Most professional and personal development tools are designed to accommodate this approach. You find your "true north," whether it be a specific vision of success, or purpose, or "why?" and set off with a map in one hand and a compass in the other to reach that destination. This framework is so ingrained in Western education and professional and personal development circles that we have come to believe that a person with many interests and talents cannot succeed unless they know where they are going before they begin and pick a lane to get there as quickly as possible—preferably at scale. Thank goodness Leonardo da Vinci didn't take that advice!

Yet, as the demands and expectations of professional and personal life shift in ways that require all of us to adapt to persistent changes and reimagine what it means to live a good life, even people who would love to pick a lane are finding that they need to diversify their practices and approaches to meet the needs of a changing environment. This means expanding beyond old paradigms and reflecting upon what it means to flourish in a world where much is unknown, challenges abound, and what is possible is yet to be imagined. It also requires us to consider new—and perhaps return to old—ways

Unfortunately, we rarely think about how we learn and what practices we need to develop to create effective learning spaces for ourselves.

of being, learning and knowing. Unfortunately, we rarely think about how we learn and what practices we need to develop to create effective learning spaces for ourselves. This is not surprising, since most of us were raised in learning environments where what we learn and how we learn it was prescribed by a teacher, a syllabus, or a program. As a result, we do what Ashley did—gather books and resources only to find ourselves overwhelmed with knowledge without a clear sense of how to apply it in practice.

"Can I read more on your website?" students, clients, mentees and others ask me once they embrace the notion that a What Now? Moment is an invitation to deeper inquiry. "Is there a course I can take?" I understand the desire to have a roadmap when the way forward is unclear, and a guide to show us the way. But finding the *right* product or service will not clear away the fog of uncertainty and light our path forward when we're navigating change. Of course we've been conditioned to believe differently. Whether in the slick offerings of a "success industrial complex" that promises bigger, better, faster ways to shape our careers and find success, or a "wellbeing industrial complex" that claims to hold the secret to a healthy and happy life, finding our way is contextual—and learning is personal.

Unfortunately, no matter how many tools, approaches and frameworks these multi-billion-dollar industries have to offer, there's no roadmap for exploring uncharted territory—it's mysterious, wild and a little bit risky. Despite the marketing promises, there is no single, cleanly packaged, off-the-shelf approach designed for mass appeal at scale that will fit all, or even most, people in the vastly varied circumstances you or your team or your family or your community face in your individual context on a day-to-day basis. Even the most well-researched model or framework can't do that work for us or offer us a turn-key solution.

That's why, rather than espouse a particular way of navigating, I encourage you to develop your own approach, built on your own principles, trusted resources, exploration, and circumstances. That means engaging in a process of rigorous self-awareness and observation of the world around you in order to explore where your aspirations and ambitions intersect with the needs of others at work, at home, in your community and across the globe. It also points to a collection of skills and capacities that we rarely discuss that are imperative for navigating uncharted territory—sensemaking, wayfinding and discernment, which we will discuss in the next two sections.

For now, as we consider what we've learned from allowing ourselves to stop, temper our incendiary emotions, gather the resources we need, and intentionally open up a liminal learning space where we can inquire further, it is important to acknowledge that we stand on a threshold between where we were and where we hope to be. Moving across this uncharted territory it involves a commitment to thinking differently and a willingness to be intentional about developing an approach to learning that is aligned with the resources at our disposal and the way we approach gathering and processing information. This is a good news/bad news situation. The good news? Learning is a creative act that can be approached in a variety of ways. The bad news? Folding new information into existing frameworks and paradigms can be more troublesome than we think. That's why having the humility to acknowledge that we have something to learn and the willingness to become teachable when we choose to meet uncertainty with curiosity and an exploratory mindset is fundamental to learning to flourish in the face of What Now? Moments.

It is important to note here that being teachable does not mean a willingness to accept new ideas and frameworks at face value. Instead, teachability is simply a willingness to believe that new circumstances, information and contexts may require us to shift our perspective and consider new ways of being and doing to meet the moment. It involves a readiness to consider that our view is not fully formed. That there is always more to learn. That we know what we know today but are not so firm in our knowledge that we close ourselves off to new information that might allow us to see things differently. This is a bold and courageous choice because accepting "I don't know" and entering liminal learning space can be its own threat. That means you stand on a threshold with a choice to make. How will you mark the occasion?

Marking points of transition

In some cultures—current and past—the creation of rituals, rites of passage and traditions were and are commonplace ways of marking and moving over thresholds and into transition. There are so many examples that could be used here. Rites of movement into adulthood, marriage rituals, rites for grief, death and dying. But also for the changing of the seasons, hunting celebrations and others.

Unfortunately, many such traditions have been lost in the modern era. For many people, marriage is viewed as "just a piece of paper" and the equivalent of a successful hunt is a promotion from manager to director that may or may not be followed by a celebratory drink. More and more, the combination of the pace of living and the devaluing of tradition is resulting in perpetual motion and the assumption that moving forward to more, bigger and scaling, is more important than creating and participating in rituals to be more intentional about life's planned and unplanned changes. Marking our entry into and out of transitional learning spaces helps to define our container and ground us in a third space. Human beings have engaged in such rites of passage for millennia—and we might learn from the rituals of the past to understand how to create new ones that help to inform how we engage with an uncertain future.

Understanding the contours of what we know and what we don't as we move into a transition is an important factor in change that is overlooked when we stand on the threshold of liminal space. This is especially true when we are thrust into transition or find ourselves lost in a transition we did not choose. Rites of passage and milestone markers are guideposts we can rely on when passing into and through transitional learning spaces. Being clear about how we approach the liminal learning space can make or break how we navigate them. Every What Now? Moment offers the opportunity to consider whether we're on the cusp of big moves and grand changes or a time for reflection and remaining on the same path. Developing rituals to mark transitions gives us a chance to ask—do I want to bloom where I'm planted now? Should I return to a place where things were more aligned with where I want to be?

This is not a common chapter in most professional and personal development books. The chapter that says: if you are not ready, then wait. If you are not sure, then contemplate. If your dream is not a dream for now, then make it a dream for later. Authors like me are "supposed to" inspire and motivate readers to do it all and do it now.

That is not my role.

I don't want to inspire you to do more or do things differently. Instead, I'm inviting you to consider that thresholds to change are important milestones that are worthy of attention and remembrance. This is not a call to return to past rituals—although some people may choose to look to the past to find ideas. It is a call to create new ones. To create your own traditions in professional and personal spaces where you mark spaces of transition and change— even troublesome ones. These moments of reflection, action or practice provide entry points into the unknown that can lead us to places and possibilities that we might not have considered had our paths not been disrupted.

QUESTIONS FOR REFLECTION

As you consider entering liminal learning space, reflect on the following questions and find a way to capture your reflections in a way that is right for you. Write some notes, take photos, draw pictures, make a spreadsheet, record your voice or a video, start a new journal—whatever allows you to remember what you were thinking as you cross the threshold into inquiry. This can be a helpful way to create a ritual for transitions and change that you can draw upon now and in the future.

Do you feel ready, eager, and equipped?

Do you feel curious?

What is it that we are committing to?

How might you mark this place?

How might you return to it in the future?

Is there some sort of action or ritual you want to do to mark the space?

What if you decide not to proceed?

What inquiry do you need to embark upon to find out whether you are choosing to move forward or avoiding moving forward as a point of procrastination?

Are you being driven by fear or are there good and substantial reasons why you should not press forward?

Whose voice is in your head?

Do we need to resource ourselves to understand if we are embarking on our own journey or the journey that we *think* we are expected to be on?

So, as we shift from a reflective pause into inquiry—from stop to ask—be ready for anything. You may recommit to the path you are on with a reinvigorated sense of what is possible within a familiar terrain like Ashley, or consider possibilities you never imagined like Erica. By entering intentionally into inquiry, we can consider where challenges that might seem insurmountable are actually prompts to creative problem solving that can lead us in new directions. Or we may find that things we thought would be easy or quick actually require more effort and longer-term commitment than we first expected. Wherever it leads, inquiry creates space to pursue at least a cursory understanding of new terrain before driving to decide, so we can consider new possibilities and make sense of them.

This applies to changes that we choose, and those that are thrust upon us, although the latter—the three-alarm fires—can present some of the most tangled uncharted territory of all.

Inquiry creates space to pursue at least a cursory understanding of new terrain before driving to decide so we can consider new possibilities and make sense of them.

In any of these cases, moving from stop to ask is a turning point. We stand at a threshold. Think of it like a train switching yard. Many different paths forward—or sideward, or even backward to move forward. Entering liminal requires some intention and a sense of what it is that you are and are not committing to. Whether you choose to take a big step or just dip your toe in the water, making space and time to ask new questions will give you a better sense of where you are and where you hope to go.

TAKEAWAYS

- Being lost is a psychological state that is steeped in our perception of where we are and what pathways we might take to find new ways forward.

- Learning to get our bearings when we face uncharted territory is a critical threshold into transitional learning space.

- Creating rituals or rites of passage can be a helpful way of marking entry into the liminal space between What Now? and what comes next.

PART TWO

Ask

A note to the reader as you begin to 'Ask'

If you've reached this point in the *stop, ask, explore* journey you've slowed things down enough to acknowledge that What Now? Moments can be a threshold to uncharted territory. Like a hiker standing at the edge of the meadow preparing to enter a thick forest, you stand at the turning point. Do you have the will to consider new ways forward and to explore the uncertain space between What Now? and what comes next? If the answer is yes, there are three core questions to examine in order to begin making sense of the new terrain we find ourselves in and to discern how best to navigate it. The chapters in this section provide some frameworks and practices to consider as you contemplate where you are, who you are and what is possible in the wake of any What Now? Moment.

Joan

CHAPTER FIVE

Zoom in

*Rigorous self-awareness and making sense
of new terrain*

Have you ever walked into a restaurant and wondered: "Do
we seat ourselves or wait to be seated?"

We've all experienced it in one context or another. The low-
stakes yet awkward moment when you enter an unfamiliar space
and aren't quite sure what to do next. It may not be a restaurant.
The same happens in the lobby of a building. A hospital. A
school. In fact, the purpose of a lobby and all of the signage we
typically find there is to invite people into a space and help them
understand how best to navigate it. The placement of those signs
and other signals of where to go and what to do when we enter
a space is the little-known but important purview of wayfinding
professionals. In this context, wayfinding refers to "the spatial
organization of a setting" (Passini, 1996). These unsung heroes
are the people who create the flow we follow in physical spaces—
say when we enter a park or land at an airport.

When wayfinders do their job well, we don't notice it. We turn the corner in the labyrinth of hospital hallways and take for granted that there is a sign on the wall or hanging from the ceiling, right where we need it, telling us what step to take next. We come over a rise while hiking and see the white spray-painted strike on a tree or other mark just before we would have started to wonder if we'd missed something or were off track. Whether or not we would use that term for it, we also rely on organizational and cultural wayfinders to guide us on our professional and personal journeys. Onboarding processes, training programs, handbooks and other guidance help people to orient themselves and find pathways forward in their careers. Advisors, administrators and educators provide wayfinding services for learners. Cultural norms, traditions and rituals provide wayfinding clues for how we engage with our friends, families and in our communities.

Or do they?

As new technologies, processes and approaches to working, living and learning change, these imperfect, yet consistent sources of wayfinding cues are shifting from top down to bottom up. Rather than rely on employers, institutions or systems to tell us where to go and what to do, people increasingly view the trajectory of their careers and lifestyles as theirs to imagine and bring to life. This is great news, especially for people who were marginalized or otherwise not well served by the systems that defined the 20th century. It also shifts the role of wayfinder somewhere between individuals and organizations, leaving fundamental gaps in vision and practices that make sense on both sides of the equation.

As a result, individuals can no longer take for granted that there will be a sign or a signal around the corner to guide their way—or that we can plan the journey of one domain of our life without considering the implications for another. At the same time, leaders need to reimagine what it means to partner with the people who they rely on to sustain their organizations by focusing on their needs and aspirations in and outside of work. This is uncharted territory, which means we all need to learn to become our own wayfinders in and out of work—especially when we find ourselves in the liminal space between clear-cut career paths and the abstraction we frequently refer to as the "future of work."

As we move further away from long-term relationships between employees and organizations toward a more nomadic workforce, people can no longer take for granted that there will be a sign or a blaze to show them which way to turn on the path toward their own professional and personal flourishing. Unfortunately, since the hand of the wayfinder in modern life is intentionally invisible, many people credit their own sense of direction rather than the skillful placement of signs and markers for the ability to find their way. This leaves us vulnerable to disorientation and confusion when we find ourselves outside the domain of well-defined pathways to find the best way into, through, and beyond this uncharted territory.

As we move from top-down, hierarchical systems to ones where individuals, teams and groups have more autonomy to find their own way with the support of the organization rather than at the direction of the organization, the need to develop wayfinding skills and support others as they do the same is a 21st-century imperative. Thus, it is more important than ever for people to understand where the signs and signals we see are coming from and what it takes to make sense of them—especially in the context of how we choose to navigate our professional and personal lives.

As we reimagine and renegotiate the systems, structures and norms that drive culture across the globe, and employ new technology and approaches to guide our paths at work and at home, the onus of finding our way falls increasingly on us as individuals and communities. This is compounded in consumer-based cultures where the spirit of creating personalized experiences that meet our unique and particular needs in context means we have a constant stream of new options and are tasked with making sense of complex sets of choices that can be overwhelming, even when we welcome them. In formal and informal education and training settings in particular, learners are encouraged to develop their own pathways and follow them in their own way at their own pace. Family and community cultures have shifted, allowing multiple acceptable pathways for partnering, child-rearing and living arrangements. Ideas about what it means to be successful or the ways of pursuing a career trajectory have moved from particular paths driven by family expectations or a "corporate ladder" and allow for freedom to traverse a corporate lattice as we gather skills from in and outside of companies and develop personal narratives on how they come together and why our disparate skills apply in varied circumstances. Even in a grocery store, customers can choose to order online, engage with a cashier, or do self-checkout.

All of this freedom to pave our own way of being and doing in this new world is very exciting. It can also be disorienting, especially since most of us were educated in systems that not only didn't teach wayfinding skills—they discouraged them. As a result, this increasingly popular, "if you build it, they will find their way" mentality ignores the invisible role that wayfinding traditionally played in helping us to find our bearings and stay oriented. It also misses the lack of training and skill building we've done individually, among leaders and in our learning organizations in this regard. Because so much of that direction came from the invisible hand of the structures and rule-makers, we miss that wayfinding is not "human nature" but is a capacity that we need to develop in ourselves and support in those we hope to serve in our organizations, families and communities.

Unfortunately, even if we are committed to finding or helping others to find a helpful route to education, training and retraining, the wayfinding tools to do so are woefully lacking. Too often we rely on a Google search that spits back a million results, the first few pages of which are populated by the offerings of skillful marketers selling learning programs. In a conversation with an HR leader for a global media firm during a several-day leadership retreat I facilitated several years ago they admitted that, while they were quite proud of all the training and development content they'd curated in their intranet, their people weren't using it at all. When I asked some of the attendees if they used it and why, they said they were not sure where to start. There were too many choices. They were busy. And making sense of it felt like a chore, so they left it alone.

Isn't this just common sense?

"Wait a minute," readers over 40 may be thinking. "Nobody taught me how to do this. Wayfinding is just common sense."

According to Webster's dictionary, common sense consists of knowledge, judgment and taste, which is more or less universal and which is held more or less without reflection or argument. So, if you find yourself in a homogeneous environment where most people agree upon the way things are done (the most simplified definition of culture) and you embrace the hand of the invisible wayfinders to guide your steps, it's easy to believe that what's popular and familiar to you is "common sense." In the 20th century, what was popular and familiar in many Western cultures was aspiring to have a good job, a "traditional" family, a nice house, and to live a nice life. Moving up in a company was not about choosing multiple paths upward—it was climbing a prescribed ladder. Moving from position to position across firms or industries was "job hopping," not skill and experience gathering. Choosing alternative family arrangements and making decisions about fertility was uncomplicated, not freezing eggs and IVF. We didn't see the guidance of cultural wayfinders because they were simply the system in which we had been born and were conditioned to operate within. We don't always see it now in the form of algorithms, influencers and technologies built to nudge us in one direction or another.

As the cultural norms that once guided our professional and personal paths are dismantled and reimagined, the task of finding our way through a company, a career, a community, a life involves unlearning identities, reconsidering old habits, rethinking existing power structures, reimagining what work means to us, and reflecting upon what it means to live a good life—all while keeping up with the abstract but much-discussed "lifelong learning." Unfortunately, many of the people I've worked with over the past decade report that they feel ill-equipped for this complex task. That's because reflecting on who we are, what we hope for and exploring how we might bring those hopes to life involves more than identifying your strengths, finding your "why?" or building a particular set of skills. It involves developing practices, principles and frameworks that can help us to know who we are and how we fit across different contexts and circumstances as those contexts and circumstances are constantly shifting and changing. I think this is what Owen Muir, M.D. was talking about when we discussed the pivot metaphor and he nodded to the challenge people face as we try to find our self-world fit.

Wayfinding and the self-world fit

Understanding who we are (identity) and where we hope to go (self-direction) are key orientation points when we engage in wayfinding in the context of navigating uncertain transitions. Despite how helpful it can be to draw upon stories and principles of navigating in physical spaces to understand being lost in transition, finding tangible markers and guideposts to help navigate liminal learning spaces is more elusive.

Employing tactics like developing rites and rituals or engaging with metaphors can help us to construct guideposts to orient ourselves as we move in and out of liminal spaces and seek to find *alignment between our perception of self and our environment— our self-world fit*. When that alignment is off it can contribute to feelings of being lost and disoriented, which can prevent us from entering liminal learning spaces. When our self-world fit feels more in alignment, we can be more adventurous, learning, exploring and experimenting, and less likely to view change as a threat.

Unfortunately, our self-world fit can come ajar when we encounter What Now? Moments. That's what happened to Andrea Bussell. Andrea left her position as a successful communications professional at a high-profile cultural institution in New York City to take a job she knew wasn't right for her from the day she accepted it. She told me, "They recruited me and made such a strong offer that it seemed like an interesting next step. But almost immediately, it became clear to me that I'd landed in a toxic and chaotic startup culture that was unaligned with my values and left me little room to perform to the best of my skills and expertise." She knew she was a creative spirit at heart with a deep desire to find work that aligned with her love of nature, but as the Covid-19 pandemic intensified, she found herself living alone in a tiny Brooklyn studio apartment working

Understanding who we are (identity) and where we hope to go (self-direction) are key orientation points when we engage in wayfinding in the context of navigating uncertain transitions.

FIGURE 5.1 Self-world fit

from home 16 hours a day on projects that didn't inspire her. "I just kept dreaming of being in the forest somewhere and was trying to come up with a way to make that happen realistically. I knew I wanted to leave New York, but I was conflicted because I'd built a life there for 17 years." On top of that, her relationship with her partner was imploding, so she was experiencing a What Now? Moment across professional and personal domains.

Once we temper the threat response that this sort of complex, multi-dimensional What Now? Moment often sparks, deeper questions emerge. For Andrea, that meant opening an inquiry into broader possibilities than she'd considered previously. For others it involves questioning who they are and what matters to them after being "downsized" or wondering what their place is in an organization where their team or department is merged with another. In each case and countless others, rigorous self-awareness is a helpful stepping-off point for getting as clear a picture as possible of the "self" in self-world fit.

Why start with rigorous self-awareness?

Self-awareness is a critical part of orienting ourselves in the world. How we identify ourselves and how we are viewed by others can play a big part in how we make sense of the world and place ourselves in it. We've talked about how destabilizing and disorienting interruptions and disruptions can be and how they can call our identity into question. Who am I if I don't get a good job when I graduate? Who am I if my skills are no longer vital in a changing economy? Who am I if I have this child? Who am I if I decide to go back to school or close my business? Too often we ask these kinds of questions on rotation in our heads rather than actually address them as creative prompts. As a result, they become ruminations rather than invitations to inquiry. This is a missed opportunity to gather helpful information that can contribute to our wayfinding efforts.

Organizational psychologist Tasha Eurich calls self-awareness the meta-skill of the 21st century, and defines it as "the ability to see ourselves clearly—to understand who we are, how others see us, and how we fit into the world around us." Of course, the pursuit of self-understanding goes much deeper and further back than a 21st-century thought leader. As a species, human beings have spent millennia trying to understand how we fit in the world and what it means to live a good life. This is not surprising since, as Eurich suggests, "when we see ourselves clearly, we are more confident and more creative. We make sounder decisions, build stronger relationships, and communicate more effectively" (Eurich, 2017). Moreover, there are moral implications, such as decreased likelihood that we will lie, cheat and steal, and we are "more effective leaders with more satisfied employees and more profitable companies" (Eurich, 2017).

Seeing ourselves as clearly as possible with the information and insight we have at our disposal is particularly important when we enter liminal space and engage in liminal learning. Like someone lost in the wilderness, finding what direction to walk is only part of the information you need to reorient yourself and find your way. Your approach to finding your way is as much built on who you are in the moment as it is where you are. Are you injured? Are you in shock? Can you trust your judgment? Do you have any impediments you need to consider before you walk on? You might approach the task of finding your way out of the wilderness differently if you had a twisted knee. You wouldn't take a route across a river if you don't know how to swim. You might make poor decisions if you're in shock. Understanding your own strengths, weaknesses and vulnerabilities in the moment helps to determine the best way over, under or around the barriers to progress that come your way.

Research suggests that most of us don't know ourselves very well, even though we think we do. This leaves us in the dark to strengths we can maximize and vulnerabilities we can gather resources to support. By taking what some call a fearless and searching look at who we are and what we hope for, we have information with which to orient ourselves and set course. We began this process in Chapter 2 with the resilience wheel by reflecting on what potential points of resistance might help us to temper our incendiary emotions and knee-jerk reactions when we face What Now? Moments. Knowing what kind of situations and circumstances tend to get under our skin and spark the threat response gives us a better chance of recognizing incendiary emotions, tempering them, gaining our composure, and moving from reaction to a dispassionately curious response. But self-awareness is about more than where we are vulnerable to threat. What matters to us, what professional and personal roles we hope to play, how our aspirations intersect with the needs of others in our lives, communities, workplaces, and the world at large—these are more complex questions that invite deeper reflection and integration across the domains of our professional and personal lives.

Rigorous self-awareness in practice

Whether we embrace the promise of uncharted territory as an opportunity or a challenge (or maybe a little bit of both), understanding the terrain we're in and choosing the path we want to take involves developing guiding principles from the inside out rather than relying solely on cultural norms and societal dreams to guide the way. That is why zooming in and committing to a practice of rigorous, honest self-awareness is a key capacity for 21st-century life. So, how do we move from trite calls to follow our passion or ideals of living meaningfully to opening an intentional inquiry into what makes us tick? What resources do we need to do so in ways that are both healthy and productive?

As mentioned previously, there is no shortage of books, blogs, podcasts, personality tests and other assessment tools we can use to learn more about ourselves. We can also connect with therapists, coaches, educators and others dedicated to professional and personal development. We have created industries around tools, frameworks and resources designed to help us identify strengths, clarify our identities, manage our time and build new capacities to deal with change. Some of them are wonderful. Others are less helpful. Rather than add another tool to the mix, I suggest you consider using what you've already done to make sense of what you know, what you don't know, and how you might fill in the gaps.

This helps keep us from zig-zagging from solution to solution in search of the "right" tool to "answer" the question of who we are, as if we are doing market research. Instead, we can develop a practice of self-inquiry, built on approaches that align with our capacities, interests and aspirations. It places us in an orientation of discovery rather than problem solving. Engaging with self-inquiry in this way liberates us from moving from tool to tool looking for a quick fix. It also alleviates the guilt and frustration many people experience when we feel forced or obligated to engage with practices and tools that do not resonate. If you are a leader or an educator, it may also be helpful to encourage those you serve to go beyond simply accumulating certificates and taking courses and provide them with resources to make sense of what they've actually learned about, who they are, and how they hope to show up at work and beyond. You might even bring a practice of inquiry and sensemaking into your development practices and reviews as a means to encourage people to think about what matters to them and how they can bring those values, ambitions and motivations to bear in the organization.

Where to start?

Whether you are working on your own or with others, inquiry begins with an intentional exploration of our inner terrain, and there is no single "right way" to approach it. Many readers will come to this book having spent years developing practices to explore who they are and what makes them tick. Others will be new to it. Either way, the focus here is less on how we respond when things are going our way. In this context, we're focusing on how you respond to the What Now? Moment in front of you—and that response can be surprising. Disruptions and interruptions can bring out the best, the worst or the unexpected in all of us. Timid people can be uncharacteristically brave—and otherwise courageous people can become timid in the face of one sort of uncertain transition. Those same people can go the other way when the transition context and risk factors change. That's why it is can be helpful to take a clear-eyed snapshot of your current state whenever you face a What Now? Moment, without making assumptions based upon previous responses to change. This prompts an inquiry into the now and into ourselves as we relate to the world around us in a particular context. No aspiration. No ideals. No "I wish I was." A simple, but rigorous, examination of where you are today—with all the warts, scars and half-baked parts of the cake we bring to where we stand. This can help you to identify a grounding point for navigation. The current state mapping exercise below can be a helpful tool to get you started.

EXERCISE Current state mapping

Mapping where we are at the beginning of our inquiry can help to ground us in the current reality before we wander too far in uncharted territory. This doesn't need to take long, nor does it need to be "complete." This is just an opportunity to capture a snapshot of the transition terrain as you see it from the vantage point of where you begin your exploration. There are no right or wrong answers—and identifying what you don't know is as important as capturing what you do know. You can return to this exercise again and again as you proceed with your inquiry. You can then use some of these reflections, insights from the resilience wheel, your metaphors and other observations and information you have to make sense of where you are and where you hope to go. Keep in mind that you can collect these reflections in any form—analog or digital. Make it your own. Also, please resist the urge to categorize or understand (more on that in Chapter 7). Simply reflect, capture and create, and you'll have a great place to start.

- **Activity Map**: Reflect on your current activities and create a visual representation that reflects how you currently spend your time (at work, outside of work, online, etc.). Use your calendar, diary, or any other tools to capture as thoroughly as possible how you currently spend your time.

- **Skills Map**: Reflect on your current skills and create a skills map. These may be professional skills, personal skills, or things you can do that have seemingly no relationship to what we are doing here. Think about times you have been proud of an outcome and what you were doing, whether or not it seems relevant to our work together. Again, please don't censor yourself.

- **Influence Map**: Reflect on your current sphere(s) of influence and create a visual representation that shows all individuals, groups, organizations, online communities, etc. where you hold any amount of influence—large or small. These may be areas where you love having influence, or ones where you wish you didn't. Please do not censor yourself. Include them all.

- **Impact Map**: Reflect on your current sense of things. What do you hope to know, do, change, impact in the world? Your life? For yourself? For others? What legacy do you hope to leave? What needle do you want to move in your home, your community, at work, in the world? Identify these boldly (think big picture!) without censoring yourself.

- **Barriers Map**: Reflect on your current sense of what is in your way. What is missing? Where are you under-resourced? What isn't working? What are the stress points? The pain points?

- **Resource Map**: Reflect on your current sense of the resources available to you. What is working? Where are you well-resourced? What are the strong points? The points of joy?

Start making sense

As we populate these maps, the terrain of our transitional learning space begins to take shape. Looking at the maps you'll begin to see what resources you have, whether or not they feel complete. Aspirations for where you want to go may emerge, whether or not you have clarity of what is ahead of you. You may have the impulse to quickly assess the content of the maps and move forward, but the purpose of this exercise is to understand the new terrain and acknowledge that we have entered uncharted territory. Here's where I begin. X marks this spot. I can choose to go forward. I can choose to go back. I can stay right here where I am—or I need to find another possibility. This is my best understanding and estimation of my circumstances, and I am ready to commit to a deeper inquiry and process of sensemaking before I decide my next move.

There is a deep rabbit hole you can go down if you want to learn more about sensemaking in theory and practice. Researchers and practitioners deliberate and debate about what sensemaking is and how it can be applied to understand where we are and where we are heading in changing times. I find these perspectives fascinating, and highly encourage anyone to avail themselves of the sensemaking resources at the end of the book to learn more about how to take your interest further (see Appendix E). For our purposes, in the context of using these skills to find our way day-to-day in professional and personal life, we draw upon a combination of natural sensemaking skills we already rely on to navigate the spaces we inhabit, and build upon them through observation, inquiry, and trial and error.

Let's begin with an important point. All of us already have the fundamental capacity to be sensemakers and wayfinders. These are innate human skills that come so naturally to us in some domains that we take them for granted. This is a missed opportunity to recognize an inherent strength we all share and engage that strength intentionally in circumstances and contexts where it does not come naturally by default. It takes attention and practice and a dispassionate curiosity about what it means to make sense of things and how a sensemaking practice might support your wayfinding efforts. Thankfully, there is no single way to make sense of things. Sensemaking is much more of an art than a science, so, rather than focus on a single definition of sensemaking, I invite you to think about sensemaking as one of many practices we can engage when a What Now? Moment throws us off course. In that moment of threat, we can practice the art of intentional inquiry. "I don't know what to do!" can shift to questions like, "How am I doing?" "Where am I stuck?" and "How might I connect to the emotional, physical, material and social resources I need to get my bearings and reorient myself?" In doing so, we move from saccharine calls to "get curious" to an engaged inquiry — dispassionate curiosity in action.

This approach invites you or your team to develop your own capacity to make sense of the unfamiliar and navigate it based upon your own constellation of aspirations, values, resources, relationships, and other considerations that are unique to you and the situation in which you find yourself. You have the capacity for sensemaking in you. We all do. But you can also build your sensemaking capacity and develop a practice of gathering observations and seeking to make sense of them as a vehicle to sensemaking.

Sensemaking wayfinding and wayfinding as sensemaking

As we've discussed throughout this book, we know we are living in a tumultuous age marked by persistent and enduring change. On the one hand, everything is different from previous generations. Opportunities have increased tenfold thanks to technology and other advancements, and along with those new opportunities come a myriad of complex situations and decisions we might not have faced in different times. Yet on the other hand, the ways in which we form communities, grow, change and learn, seek meaning and purpose, and share wisdom with those who come next are remarkably similar to those who came before us. Ultimately, despite the shifts that require us to rethink everything, we humans are born, grow, change, become—and then we go. Just like our ancestors did. For all the answers we've found about the world around us, the core questions of what it means to be human—what it means to live a good life, how we're meant to be—remain equally interesting and largely unanswered. With all the technology and advancements of the past few centuries, we are engaging with ancient questions in new contexts.

Rather than seek to answer these kinds of questions in a deep or profound way, however, we often work them out through mundane and practical questions, like what we should do for a living. So, finding our purpose or seeking meaning becomes something that is in service to professional or personal wayfinding. When we face professional and personal turning points, we are not only called to reconsider where we should go and how we should get there (direction), we are also called to consider who we are (identity) and how we choose to live (presence). This is true of us as individuals and in community, at work and beyond. Making sense of these aspects of life and how they relate to our self-world fit—or having a confidence that we can develop approaches to learn—is not only a fundamental part of being human, but is also at the core of developing a wayfinding practice that is grounded in sensemaking.

We observed this on a global scale during the Covid-19 pandemic, when challenging circumstances were coupled with a deep and prolonged pause. All but the front-line workers among us were prevented from distracting ourselves with typical day-to-day activities and found ourselves asking deeper questions than we might have done otherwise. But we don't have to wait for these kinds of massive existential events to engage with deep inquiry. Even the most mundane What Now? Moments can, if we let them, become more than points of decision. These milestones along our journey can become catalysts of our own becoming and the becoming of the organizations, projects, and endeavors we have set out to create.

So, if you enter into liminal learning spaces with an eye on learning to make sense of who you are and what is possible in your unique and complex circumstances—you can identify a broad set of options that can help you maintain a sense of direction.

But it doesn't stop there. We need to consider what we learn in our practice of rigorous self-awareness in the contexts we share with others and recognize that where we bring our aspirations to life also offer clues and insights that are useful for wayfinding. That is why wayfinding is not a set of steps we follow. As with the wilderness explorers we've discussed throughout the text, it is a continual process of learning in action and a willingness to continually calibrate and recalibrate as we gather new information and fold what we learn in times of inquiry and exploration into times of execution. We do this by wayfinding

If you enter into liminal learning spaces with an eye on learning to make sense of who you are and what is possible in your unique and complex circumstances— you can identify a broad set of options that can help you maintain a sense of direction.

from the inside out (zooming in) and bringing what we learn into context, so we are also wayfinding from the outside in (zooming out).

TAKEAWAYS

- Rigorous self-awareness provides a grounding point for our wayfinding journey as we enter uncharted territory.
- Finding our self-world fit can be a point of orientation as we engage in a process of sensemaking and wayfinding.
- Mapping our current state is a helpful stepping-off point for inquiry.

CHAPTER SIX

Zoom out

Wayfinding from the outside in

"So, what do you hope for?" I ask this question frequently of my students, clients, and research participants when they're feeling lost or unsettled.

"I just want to be happy."

"I want to do something meaningful."

"I want to follow my passion."

"I want to be famous."

"I want to make money."

"I want to change the world."

All perfectly reasonable, but not very helpful when it comes to orienting or reorienting ourselves in uncertain transitions. That becomes crystal clear when I follow up with the second set of questions.

"What makes you happy and what route do you plan to take to pursue it?'

"What do you find meaningful and how might you bring meaning into your life both professionally and personally?"

"What are you passionate about and how does that relate to the way you walk through the world on a daily basis?"

"How much money and fame are enough and how will you know when you've arrived?"

"What change do you want to bring to the world and what makes you think you are the right person to bring it?"

Shifting from ideal outcomes to specific, grounded questions about how we intend to bring our ideals to life on a day-to-day basis moves the wayfinding question from theory to practice, and it is a place where many people get stuck. Hoping to find our way back to the car when we're lost in the woods, or to find an oasis in the desert, is very different than knowing what route to take to get there. That's why zooming in to focus on rigorous self-awareness *and* zooming out to develop a deep understanding of the context in which we are operating are both crucial parts to finding our way.

When we move from ideals to action in the context of an uncertain transition, we quickly see that there are many ways to pursue joy or happiness, to do meaningful work or to make a good living—even when we feel constrained by limited time, resources or opportunity. If we rely solely on self-awareness to guide our way, we can risk making ourselves and our own needs, wants and desires the central point of orientation for wayfinding. If we overcorrect in the other direction, we can make more worldly concerns our central point of orientation for wayfinding and become too focused on the expectations or needs of others, which can throw us off course. By looking both inside and out, we can avoid the trap that so many good-hearted people fall into—focusing on ourselves to the detriment of others or focusing on others to the detriment of ourselves. Finding and maintaining a sustainable balance between the two is like a dance where one partner moves with the other and anticipates where the other is headed—sometimes before they know themselves. When it flows, it can be magical. When it doesn't, we may step on some toes and need to try again. In either case, this is at the heart and soul of our pursuit of wayfinding.

Wayfinding fundamentals

In Chapter 5 I described wayfinding as the system of signs, maps and other navigation systems that guide us through spaces (see Appendix F for more on wayfinding). In the navigation of physical spaces, that is called *aided wayfinding* and it includes tools like GPS and other navigation assistants that help make finding our way less ambiguous (see Figure 6.1). Despite the changing shape of work, there are still fields and firms where aided wayfinding still exists in the form of prescribed paths and roadmaps to "climb the corporate ladder." The military, law enforcement, emergency services and government service are some good examples. Some areas of healthcare, teaching and professional services are some others. In each of these industries, there remain some prescribed routes for advancement that follow a particular path or trajectory—at least for now.

FIGURE 6.1 Aided wayfinding

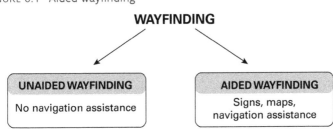

Adapted from Wiener et al, 2004

People in these fields encounter What Now? Moments along the way, but they are more likely to be potholes or detours. When people operate in systems that have retained those 20th-century models, uncharted territory still exists, but it typically comes when we enter or leave the organization, rather than from inside it. The year I accepted the position my father was so thrilled about at Con Edison, the average tenure of a person at the company was 34 years. The people I worked with made one career decision in their late teens or early twenties and received their paycheck from one organization until the day they retired. Career paths were set by human resources departments, union contracts and organization charts that were fixed and predictable for people who got their foot through the door, and major life events were driven by cultural norms and traditions. The point of orientation and desired outcome remained clear, even when things went wrong in the day-to-day. It is increasingly rare for 21st-century work and life trajectories to unfold in that way.

Unaided wayfinding

In unaided wayfinding there is no navigation assistance. No maps, signs or GPS. This is the empty beach, the gig economy career trajectory we've discussed previously (see Figure 6.2). When we step outside the signs, systems and structures that prescribe a set trajectory for our work, our life, our business or our strategy, we have the freedom to go our own way. Like a person who enters the woods for a hike and chooses to step off the trail and explore outside of what's already been blazed. There is freedom in this approach, of course, but also greater uncertainty and potential to become lost or turned around because we are finding our own way. We can view that distinction as a reason to stick to set paths, which can feel like the safe bet until we hit a barrier to progress and face a What Now? Moment. In these cases, the way forward is ours to discern. As a result, clarifying

FIGURE 6.2 Unaided wayfinding

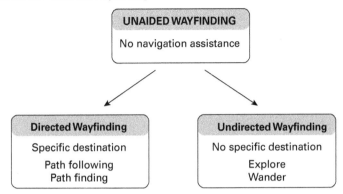

Adapted from Wiener et al, 2004

what we do or don't know about where we hope to go and possible routes to get us there can illuminate possible next steps, even if we are unsure of the specific outcome we seek. Unfortunately, despite an increasing need for unaided wayfinding skills in our personal and professional lives, most people have received little instruction in the topic.

Directed wayfinding

There are two types of unaided wayfinding: directed and undirected. When we engage in *directed wayfinding* we have a specific destination in mind and the primary task at hand is to find (or create) a path that leads to the intended destination. Sometimes we know where we hope to go, but don't have an established path or milestone markers to guide us. Maybe we were thrown off course or we're just entering the workforce and have not yet discovered how best to bring the specific aspiration we have to life. Navigators call that directed wayfinding and it involves searching for what we hope for, following when a path shows up in front of us, and seeking new paths to arrive at a chosen destination. In practice this can involve connecting with people who have arrived where we hope to go and learning about their paths to getting there. Or familiarizing ourselves with the terrain by immersing ourselves in it or connecting with and observing the experiences of people who are where we hope to go. We might find a job or an internship to place us in closer proximity to where we hope to be, or we can gain insights through other experiences that provide a window into a terrain we have yet to travel within.

Undirected wayfinding

Undirected wayfinding is different. This is for people like Erica, Ashley, and others who don't have a specific destination in mind. It involves exploration and roaming, which we will discuss more in Part Three. In either case, whether we have a set destination or are learning as we go, being and doing in a technology-driven world that is less hierarchical and prescriptive means we are more frequently operating in unfamiliar terrain that invites us to develop a wayfinding practice.

Wayfinding is a practice, not a product

Even though we know that the days of finding a good company and staying there for three or four decades are gone, many people—even students in their late teens and early twenties—are nostalgic for a time when career and life paths were clearer from the onset. People embrace the ideal of gaining new skills, experiences and networks, and becoming willing to learn, grow, adapt and be a good problem solver, but we fall short when we face the question of how to prepare ourselves and others to bring those ideals to bear in the day-to-day. This hesitation—which can sometimes overwhelm—raises questions about how we can develop our self-direction skills and what kind of wayfinding supports and services are necessary to help people get their bearings and find their way forward in rapidly changing environments.

Before we move into deeper inquiry about what it means to engage wayfinding in this task, it is important to acknowledge that any of the wayfinding frameworks, tools or tactics I present here were created in the field with individuals and teams to equip them as they engaged with their own uncharted territory. While they have been tried and tested in a variety of contexts and scenarios, they are meant to be interacted with experimentally and adapted to meet the needs of the contexts in which they are applied. Play. Engage. Test them out and adapt them to your context—then take what works and leave what doesn't. Let's start with the hope compass, a tool that was created to help people get their bearings as they cross the threshold into uncharted territory. It has proven to be a helpful tool for grounding individuals and teams in liminal space.

And yes, I am using the H-word.

The role of hope in getting your bearings

Before the "hope is not a strategy" and "hope is wishful thinking" folks get up in arms, let's make some space for a more robust view of hope. I draw on the research of Luthans and colleagues and their conceptualization of hope as part of their psychological capital model to demonstrate a positive relationship between hope and performance (Luthans et al, 2015). In areas as varied as athletics, academia and coping for individuals, and profitability of business units and employee satisfaction and organizational commitment in organizations, finding the will and the motivation to search for new pathways forward has been demonstrated to lead to increased energy and a sense of control that often results in an upward spiral of hope (Rand et al, 2009). While I am sure there are philosophers, theologians and social scientists who might balk at the practicality of this view of an ancient concept, for our purposes, commanding our own agency and pointing it in the direction of a pathway to change provides a very helpful framework for thinking about hope in the context of feeling stuck or lost on the threshold of an uncertain transition. In particular, their characterization of hope as *willfinding* and *wayfinding* speaks to what it takes to set off on a journey into uncharted territory.

Hope compass

It is important to note that the hope compass I present here (see Figure 6.3) is not designed to point you to true north. Nor is it designed to be a sure-fire way of finding yourself, your purpose, or your "why?". In fact, while we've used navigation references throughout this book, this compass is more like the primitive compasses that appeared in China around the 4th century BC than those we picture today. Those early compasses were less geared toward navigation in physical spaces (although they could be used for that purpose). Instead, they are said to have been used to help people uncover insights into how they might order and harmonize their environments and their lives (Merrill et al, 1983). While the hope compass is not a tool that promises to help you find success or wellbeing, it can be a useful orienting tool in the face of uncertainty.

The first and most important thing to remember as you engage with the hope compass is that, like any compass, there is no single way to use it—and it won't tell you where to go. It won't lead you in a specific direction and it doesn't have an ideal destination in mind for you.

And neither do I.

The tool simply provides a place to begin to get your bearings when the way forward is unclear and you are unsure how to begin thinking about it. This can be applied to big questions, like "should I change careers?", or mundane ones, like "should we take this new client?". Unlike tools designed to drive progress and growth, this is particularly suited to liminal spaces and What Now? Moments, because it prompts reflection across domains.

FIGURE 6.3 Hope compass

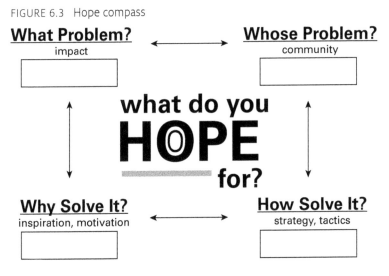

What do you hope for?

There is something very provocative about pondering the question of what we hope for. It feels lofty and abstract, neither of which are typically valued or rewarded in professional settings. Perhaps it's a little more acceptable in personal settings, but it's still a less than concrete starting place for execution and planning. That's what makes it so useful in liminal space. Pondering what we hope for and how we might move toward it allows us to zoom out and consider a direction without fully defining a precise outcome. It is a point of orientation rather than a point of execution. It also serves as a very helpful guidepost for reflecting on what matters and grounding ourselves and our teams in inquiry when we stand on the threshold of a new project or are tentative about how to approach a new challenge.

QUESTION FOR REFLECTION

Think about a challenge or turning point you are facing now. Reflect on the before, during and after and consider the question: what do you hope for?

The problem with problem solving

Before we dig further into the hope compass, I offer a cautionary critique of its problem-solving orientation. If we are not careful, viewing wayfinding as a problem to solve can lead us to a mindset that everything is a problem and we can miss opportunities. The old "if you're a hammer, everything is a nail" adage. That said, when people find themselves entering liminal space (or lost in it) they tend to view the initial inquiry as a problem to solve, which means that many people find the problem-solving orientation to be helpful. So, in the same way that a good carpenter creates their own tools, I encourage you to change the words in the framework to better match your metaphors or your circumstances if it makes it more useful to you. Like any wayfinding tool—from maps and compasses to GPS—it is imperfect. But it also provides a prompt for gaining clarity and identifying gaps in knowledge and understanding. Reflecting on these prompts provides us with a sense of who and where we are within the evolving context, before we move to solution finding and decision making. Again, we are not looking for a specific answer here. The key is to allow the hope compass to help spark reflection and inquiry, rather than get bogged down in specifics. It is another sensemaking tool that can provide us with further insight into where we are, how we are, and where we might proceed from here. It can also help identify the resources we need to engage with the challenge (or opportunity) at hand.

Another note. While I will walk you through the compass to help you become familiar with it, this is not a one-off exercise. You will likely return to this tool over and over again, in the same way you might pull a more modern compass or your GPS out of your pocket as you move in and out of orientation and disorientation on a long journey. As such, it is better understood in use than it is as described. I hope you will take it off the page and learn from it rather than learn about it. That said, here goes...

What's your problem and how do you solve it?

Whether we're dealing with professional or personal challenges, most of us have been trained to view a swift move from problem to solution as the most efficient way to respond. It is certainly how most people I work with come to wayfinding. They arrive in liminal space convinced that they know what the problem is—the job they need to leave or the work/life balance conundrum they need to address—and they want answers. Preferably as quickly as possible. While the hope compass can be quite effective at prompting new thinking about problem solving, the route from problem to solution is not direct.

While the hope compass can be quite effective at prompting new thinking about problem solving, the route from problem to solution is not direct.

Instead, by asking a variety of questions and gathering insights across domains of inquiry, new questions and surprising insights can emerge. Often, rather than moving straight from problem to solution, the inquiry leads to clarification of the problem itself. So, rather than instinctively starting in one place, I invite you to enter the compass beginning with whichever question makes you feel most grounded in your inquiry.

Some people (you may be among them) are very clear about a particular problem they aspire to solve. This can be a manager who is having trouble with team dynamics or a graduating student who hopes to make a difference or a mid-career leader who aspires to become a top-level executive. For these people, beginning in the top left corner of the model makes sense. Don't worry if you are not clear yet. You are simply grounding yourself in your best first thought. The key to using this tool effectively is to concern yourself less with the specific answer to any one of the questions, and more with how the questions relate to one another to help to define your best thinking about your circumstance in the moment. As I mentioned earlier, these questions and how they relate to one another will raise more questions than they answer. That is fine. In the space in Figure 6.4, capture your best sense of what the problem is that you are facing.

FIGURE 6.4 What problem?

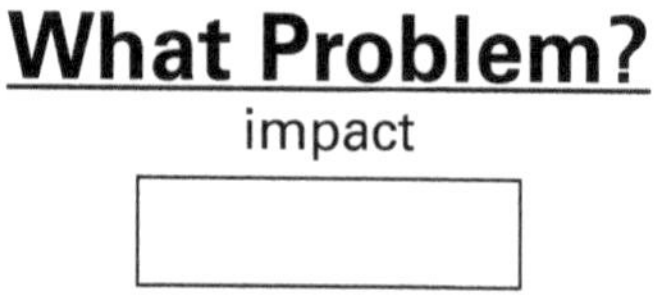

What Problem?
impact

Next, with that problem in mind, think about whose problem you seek to solve. For instance, if the problem you hope to solve is to increase sales, whose problem do you care to address? The customer's problem? The salesperson's challenge? The manager or leader who is tasked with creating strategy and tactics? As you can see from these simple prompts, the way you might go about solving that sales challenge might be very different depending upon whose problem you seek to solve. This question prompts a deeper reflection, which can help to home in on the specifics of both the problem and possible solutions. Place your thoughts on whose problem you hope to solve in the box in Figure 6.5.

FIGURE 6.5 Whose problem?

Whose Problem?
community

Contemplating why you are the right person or team to solve a problem can be a very helpful and grounding step in contemplating whether the problem we're focused on is actually ours to solve. It may seem counterintuitive at first or prompt responses like, "because it's my job" or "because I said so." It is a more nuanced and thought-provoking question than that. We all face many challenges in our professional and personal lives, so there is no shortage of directions we can turn our attention toward, especially in liminal spaces. But how do you know that you or your team are the best resources to address the challenge? How do you determine which problems are your problems to solve? Contemplating this can help us to deploy the right resources to the right problems at the right time. Be sure to think about this question in the context of your answers to other questions in the compass. As I mentioned previously, this tool is most effective when it is used as a prompt for comparing and contrasting across prompts rather than coming up with "right" answers in any single domain. Using the problem you identified above, reflect on why you or your team are meant to solve it. Place your thoughts on whose problem you hope to solve in the box in Figure 6.6.

FIGURE 6.6 Why solve it?

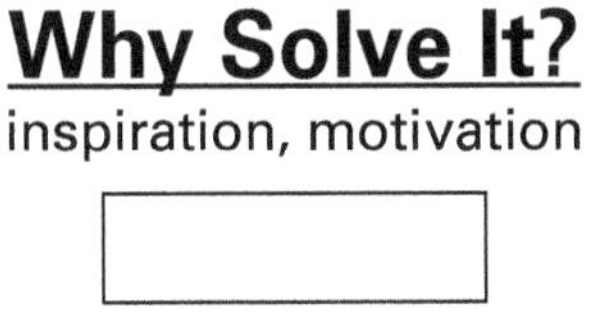

Why Solve It?
inspiration, motivation

Most teams and individuals are used to beginning by asking how to solve the problem. In fact, in some settings, we are instructed to not present a problem to the team unless we have a solution and are ready to take on the task of solving it. The hope compass offers an alternative approach that points the user to zoom out and consider the bigger picture. By considering the problem through the lens of the people doing the solving as well as those whose problem is being solved, we have a greater likelihood of making connections across the whole solutions ecosystem. Doing so through the lens of what relevant stakeholders hope for provides another layer that will shift thinking from simplified responses to a more context-based approach to creative problem solving. Now that you've considered your example across each of the prompts, think about how you might solve it and place your response in Figure 6.7.

FIGURE 6.7 How do you solve it?

How Solve It?
strategy, tactics

HOPE COMPASS IN ACTION

Tim Gilligan, a design leader at a large international financial services company, has embraced the use of the hope compass and other wayfinding tools for himself and with his team. "When we're asked to lead in design and innovation, there is no roadmap," he told me. "There are a million paths that you can take at any point of inflection. This work has really helped me coach my team on what they hope to accomplish, what they hope to be able to give or leave the team or the project with."

According to Gilligan, the value proposition of leaders tasked with leading change is not to apply best practices or rigid frameworks, but an invitation to change the system:

"The hope compass and the wayfinding mindset have helped me to coach myself and my team in a time of great change and nuance. It gives us a way to hold the adversity the business throws our way and the joy of delivering great experiences for our colleagues and customers at once. It helped create a language of experimentation, patience and curiosity in times when best practices do not apply."

The ability to focus on outcome and then navigate to that outcome using the unique values, perspectives and approaches each member of the team brings to the table has been both unsettling and liberating, Gilligan stated. "Once we got over the initial unbalancing of accepting that there is no roadmap, we were able to accept our role as the map makers. The wayfinders. And that was liberating."

A few notes

Like any other process of inquiry, the prompts in the hope compass will raise as many questions as they answer. It is designed to help you or your team to uncover what you do and don't know about your orientation (or disorientation) in this moment and where you stand against the challenges you face—whether they are major disruptions or minor interruptions. It is important to understand that, in the same way that each *What Now?* Moment is different, who we are when we encounter each of them is also different. We are growing, changing and evolving creatures with values, motivations, aspirations and commitments that change over time. Our circumstances, priorities and values may shift as we learn new things and consider new ways of being in the world—as individuals and together.

I walked through the hope compass here in a particular order, simply to give you some fundamental insight into the reasoning behind each of the prompts. As you play with the tool in your own context, be sure to remember that where you begin with the compass will completely depend upon what seems most clear to you—and that will change depending on the circumstances. "What do you hope for?" may feel like a big question you are not ready to answer at the beginning of your inquiry. You may have a deep sense of who you hope to serve, but not how you might want to serve them. You may have a deep sense of what problem you want to solve, but have never interrogated why you are the right person to solve it. Start wherever you have the most clarity. If you get stuck, choose another prompt. Whatever it takes to begin asking questions across domains and clarifying who you want to serve and how you want to serve them.

TAKEAWAYS

- Wayfinding is a nuanced process that is approached differently depending upon how clear we are on our destination and whether or not we have the tools we need to orient ourselves in uncertain spaces.

- Grounding ourselves as we move into and through inquiry is a fundamental wayfinding skill that requires a well-curated toolbox.

- The hope compass is one useful tool to help get our bearings as we navigate into and through the unknown.

CHAPTER SEVEN

What's possible?

*Identify possibilities and put
everything on the altar*

"If I handed you a 2,000-piece puzzle, how would you take it on?"
When I ask this question, most people respond in one of three
ways. "I would start with the edges," is the most common,
followed by "I sort by color" and "I look at the picture and
collect pieces related to the image."

It is rare that people give the answer I'm prompting with the
question—that nearly 100 percent of people who do a large
puzzle first dump out the pieces, spread them out on the table,
turn the pieces over and look through them before they employ
their chosen strategy to put them all together.

"Now what if the puzzle had no edges?" I ask. "Or if it were
a single color or didn't have a predetermined picture on the box
to use as a reference? How would you approach the puzzle
then?"

We rely on old or standardized processes and fail to recognize that we, our families, our organizations are evolving and changing as the context around us changes. This simple exercise is a helpful stepping-off point for taking our discussion of sensemaking in the context of wayfinding from theory to practice.

We rely on old or standardized processes and fail to recognize that we, our families, our organizations are evolving and changing as the context around us changes.

Every puzzle is a new shape—and every *What Now?* Moment is unique. When we face uncertain transitions, we often skip the fundamental step of dumping the pieces, spreading them out, turning them over and looking at them collectively to see how we want to approach the puzzle. We may like to start with the corners and edges or sort the pieces by color, but the nature of the puzzle often dictates the approach. Applied to wayfinding, the way we like to do things or feel best suited to do things does not always translate to the most effective way to approach sensemaking in a liminal context.

Pause and gather your pieces

Over the past six chapters, you've been prompted to reflect on many things related to identity, self-direction and wayfinding when we face uncertain transitions. First, your relationship with the threat response. How you react when a What Now? Moment comes your way and the importance of gathering resources to equip ourselves to navigate uncertainty. Then we considered how we reframe our thinking about points of transition through metaphor—moving from a journey metaphor to a container metaphor (basecamp), in order to define transitional learning space and, where appropriate, the time horizon for the inquiry we are opening. Once we use this reflection to compose ourselves and get our bearings we begin to inquire: where am I and who am I in this space at this time? I shared some mapping and reflective exercises that might be helpful, but also encourage you to use any tools that have worked well for you in the past to examine these questions. These can be books and other individual resources, social resources, or time with a coach or therapist or teacher or other people you know that you can rely on to get a clear picture of your current state—inside and out—whether or not you like what you see.

I return to this not as a simple wrap up of where we've been, but to underscore that all of this reflection—the bits and pieces of what we've learned as well as the gaps and holes that raise questions or point to the need for more resourcing and deeper inquiry—are the pieces of the puzzle of inquiry that we are considering in the *ask* of the *stop, ask, explore*. There is something quite important about gathering these pieces, getting them outside of our heads and having them in one place where we can see everything at once—across domains. Skipping this can compound the confusion we feel when we face uncertain transitions. Keeping all of the pieces in our heads is like trying to do a 2,000-piece puzzle without taking any of the pieces out of the box. It is possible—but it is more difficult to make sense of things and develop an approach that makes the process enjoyable rather than overwhelming and frustrating.

There are a variety of ways to approach this practice, which is less about organizing information and more about making space for sensemaking. For those of you who are used to making lists or gathering information in spreadsheets, I invite you to consider a different approach. Lists and spreadsheets have their place, of course, but they are more helpful when the objective is to manage information and drive production. In the sensemaking context, however, production-oriented tools can be limiting, in the same way that taping multiple pieces to one another would hamper completing a puzzle. Instead of organizing and categorizing, sensemaking begins with creating space to get disparate thoughts, ideas and concerns out of our heads and into a place where we can visualize them, move them around and consider different, possibly surprising, combinations and configurations. Like creating an external hard drive for recurring thoughts and concerns.

If you like to work in analog, sticky notes, index cards or other small, distinct items can be useful materials. Perhaps clear a wall somewhere in your home or office where you are willing to make a mess for a period of time. Let the ideas linger in the space in the same way you might keep a puzzle on a table. Add new thoughts and ideas as you have them. Organize and reorganize them. Let the ideas speak. You might want to carry your materials with you so you can gather new insights and ideas as they emerge. If you're using sticky notes or index cards, you can carry them in your pocket or in your bag, put some on your end table in the bedroom and have them handy in other places. This will prompt you to remain reflective and provide a convenient way to capture thoughts to add to your sensemaking space in the flow of the day, not just when you're brainstorming. For people who prefer to work digitally, there are a number of tools that can be useful for visual sensemaking. I'm particularly fond of online whiteboards like Miro and Mural as a place to easily gather and play with ideas.

Don't create categories—at least not yet!

Gathering information without categorizing is really difficult for many people because it is the polar opposite of what many of us have been taught to do. Instead, we approach our ideas in a way that is the equivalent of picking through the puzzle box to find the "right" one, as quickly and efficiently as possible, usually by narrowing it down to two or three options and choosing from among them, and often without looking at all the choices in the box. In sensemaking, we do the opposite. First, we gather all of our ideas, thoughts and other pieces in one place without compartmentalizing. This gets messy when we gather the professional and personal in one place. But the mess is worth the cost when we are able to zoom out and observe our situation holistically. It allows us to see our competing commitments clearly across and between domains.

Of course, even when I encourage people to stay away from creating themes, they laugh as they tell me that they can't help it. In part, because it's how we're trained, but also because visualizing all of the items we keep track of in lists and in our heads in one place can feel overwhelming at first. But, as you begin to see the benefits that come from capturing ideas and thoughts outside of our head before we decide how best to put them back together, the value becomes clear and the process becomes less overwhelming. Many people I work with view this part of the work as a game changer. They feel liberated from constant ruminating. As I guide people through this process, they consistently look at their sticky notes or index cards or online whiteboards and are surprised by how much information about stakeholders, stressors, dreams and fears they carry across their professional and personal worlds —and how much of a relief it can be to get it out of their heads and into a space where they can consider it in a more structured way.

When Yvette Owo, a former business strategy lead at Accenture who now owns a strategy and coaching firm, began using Miro, she called it an aha moment. "I had been at base camp for a few years. Most people around me were telling me to climb, but what I needed was to organize resources, to rest, refuel, and develop a game plan." Owo had experienced a number of high-stakes What Now? Moments, from career changes and launching a business to dealing with the aftermath of being hit by a car and mental health issues. Posting recurring thoughts on her digital whiteboard allowed her to release mental and emotional space and freed her to focus on other things. "There's something in the brain called the reticular activating system (RAS)," she told me. "It helps us keep things top of mind so we don't forget them, and also tells us what to ignore." According to Yvette, she had *tons* of things top of mind, and she found it mentally draining. "I was constantly thinking about the business. About my health. About family and personal life," she said. "From day one it was clear that my RAS was letting me release the thoughts once they were captured on the board."

Unlike others who like to have a wall or whiteboard filled with sticky notes for their ideas, Owo prefers to keep her ideas out of sight until she is ready to consider them. "I don't want to put hundreds of notes all over a wall in my home, which would then be screaming at me to do something with them," she continued. "And a list leaves me with the impression that I must do something." Instead, she puts a thought on the board and returns to it when she is ready to make sense of it. She was so pleased with the approach that she now uses it with her team to make sense of priorities, drive collaboration and identify new possibilities.

Placing all of our puzzle pieces on the table, turning them over and looking at them in all of their messy glory allows us to develop new, context-specific approaches that are more likely to carry us through.

Identify the locus of possibilities

Once the puzzle pieces you've gathered (so far) are in one place, then exploring them at once, across domains, can help us to identify surprising opportunities that might not be immediately obvious if we only explore within a single domain. It raises interesting questions about how we might create a life, organization or community of practice that not only leads to traditional variables of success, but also creates time or space for flourishing and service to others. That's what happened to Andrea, whose What Now? Moment we discussed in Chapter 5. She knew she needed and wanted to leave New York and find a career that was closer to nature, or at least a life that allowed for a deeper connection with it, but was lost in a transition she hadn't yet defined. She'd considered a few options—forestry, botany, environmental science, even becoming a park ranger—but hadn't yet watered the seeds of consideration with a wholehearted inquiry. This left her wanting, but stuck. I encouraged her to take a step in the direction of possibility by learning about all of the options that came to mind, no matter how impractical.

What would it take to be a forest ranger? What other career opportunities exist in those spaces? Do you have the skills you need, or would you need to go back to school? What resources do you have at your disposal to open up a space for active waiting? By opening up to a broad set of possibilities, Andrea began to untangle which aspects of these possibilities appealed to her in practice, and which seemed outside of her desired self-world fit.

Eventually, that initial inquiry allowed her to take some incremental steps toward her desired outcome, first by visiting family and friends for a few months in the forests of Colorado and Washington, and then to a longer stay in the Kerry mountains of Ireland. She's since moved to Stockholm and is exploring her ongoing transition from a life that was not working for her to one that feels more aligned. While expanding her personal and professional networks globally, she's been able to create more varied and creative work opportunities while living closer to nature and studying landscape photography. "I felt like I'd been shoved from the nest," she said. "Like my life was saying to me, you're not in the city you're meant to be in, you're not in the right relationship, and you're not in a job that inspires you either. So, here you go–absolute freedom and groundlessness to create from." By pursuing a wider vision, she told me, her sense of adventure and exploration was sparked and, in turn, a drive and vision she'd been lacking while living out of alignment with her authentic interests and talents was restored. "I wasn't able to see it that way without the expanse of possibility that came when everything familiar was cleared away. We live in a time where it's very possible to create your own freedom. Every person can be the entrepreneur or CEO of their own life if they expand their vision and consciousness to include multiple streams of opportunity. That's what I'm doing now."

This wider vision involves not only identifying all of the possibilities available to us, but also considering and reconsidering what matters to us with a willingness to reprioritize or remove things from consideration. Think of this like the climber entering base camp. As we discussed previously, the movement between times of climbing and times of recalibrating and resourcing at base camp are both critical parts of the climb. But base camp is about more than recalibrating the body to the right oxygen levels. It is also about considering what has changed on the last leg of the journey and what is needed for the next. This involves reflection: what items should we keep with us and what items should we leave behind and, perhaps, pick up on the way back? How is the weather on the mountain ahead? What do other climbers have to share that might be useful? That's why, if we recognize that disruptions—even painful ones—provide us with a prompt to take stock, we can consider not only the issue that caused the disruption, but also revisit every part of our lives to make sure we are properly resourced and as unburdened as we can be for the next leg of the journey. I think of this as putting everything on the altar with a willingness to let it go, no matter how precious and important it might seem.

Everything on the altar

Religions across the globe have traditions that involve sacrificing items on an altar as an act of trust, faith and commitment to that which is being honored in the rite or ritual. I view *placing everything on the altar* as a helpful metaphor for *the practice of reconsidering whether the individual elements of the careers, lives and organizations we've created are aligned with what we value and what we hope to make present in the world.*

For Andrea, this meant shifting some firm ideas about money, stability, success and other things that she still values—but recognizing that she could create a container to prioritize exploration and possibility. For others, it means intentionally letting an aspirational dream go. This was the case for another woman I worked with for about six months. "Maybe I'm not ready to pursue this dream right now," she said, looking down at her coffee and avoiding eye contact. As she described her hesitation in more detail, it was clear that this was more than a What Now? Moment threat response. Opening the Pandora's box of deep introspection and intentional examination of the layered complexities of her own life proved to be more challenging than she had originally anticipated, and she wanted to understand more about the resistance she was feeling in herself and those around her before pressing forward toward a destination that she was beginning to question.

I watched her face relax and her shoulders drop as I told her, "We are so enamored with perpetual movement and big dreams delivered at scale that we sometimes miss real opportunities to serve where we are." This gave her space to share that the aspiration she was carrying around with her had become a burden rather than a motivation. When she put it on the altar, the big dream was supplanted by a deep desire to nurture her existing customers, her community and her family rather than take things to the next level. Somehow it had not occurred to her to give herself permission to bring her dream to life in a way that felt right-sized for her at the time.

Some people are surprised when I tell them I put my marriage and family on the altar in points of transitions and turning points. It is a particularly challenging notion for "family first" people who often struggle to make sense of a transition while balancing personal commitments to partners, children, aging parents and others. I can see where they are coming from—especially since I've raised three children and been married for 25 years to my husband Martin, a man who I still view as not only a partner for life but my best friend. "How do you put that on the altar?"

I sometimes wonder if the fact that I *do* put them on the altar is what keeps things in place. So yes, at its most extreme, putting my husband on the altar means I could leave him if I chose to. While I have yet to make that choice (so far!), putting the marriage on the altar gives me the opportunity to recommit to the relationship over and over again with each point of transition. But in recommitting to the relationship, I also have the opportunity to recognize that our standing daily commitments to one another and our household might be unhelpful or problematic for my next leg of the journey. Putting something that seems immovable on the altar at a time of transition—whether relationships with family members, use of funds and savings, locations where we live, or any other variable—is a prompt to rethink that area of our lives and shift priorities intentionally to meet the moment, rather than juggle them as circumstances shift and change over time. This allows me to say to my husband, "I'm writing a book, so I need more support and will be unavailable for certain tasks—let's see how we can resource for it." It allows him to say, "I'm making this film, so I need space in the house or time out of it to devote myself to this task." Since we recognize that these reprioritizations are on a specific (and limited) time horizon and we are clear in our commitments within them, we don't have to renegotiate as we move through a project or priority. We can intentionally make the space and recalibrate as we go.

The same is true for organizations. If we normalize deploying resources in ways where we can reprioritize and adapt without making people feel threatened, we have a better chance of being the dynamic teams and organizations we say we want to be. If, instead, every shift makes people wonder who they are and if they have a place in the organization, we create systems that spark What Now? Moments that can lead to fight, flight and freeze responses that many people are unlikely to share—or even identify in themselves. Making this explicit, before a disruption that calls to change open transitional learning space where even sacred cows are put on the altar, creates a more honest and open environment for inquiry. In doing so, we can mark the shift from execution to exploration and intentionally engage active resilience and gather the resources they need to navigate the uncertain transition ahead.

This kind of preparation and transparency helps to create psychological safety and engagement, and opens up people's ability to be more creative and innovative in the spaces they inhabit. It also makes space for people to share concerns and identify areas where change feels threatening, so they can move individually and in community from the fear loop and engage dispassionate curiosity in action through sensemaking and reprioritizing across domains, where necessary.

When we make sense of disparate items to explore new possibilities, it is our tendency (and our training) to separate, categorize and explore possibilities within particular domains. What are my possibilities at work? At home? In the community? Then, after we've categorized, we might prioritize or seek to create some "balance" between areas that invite us to 100 percent focus across four or five domains. But that means we find ourselves operating at 500 percent—and we wonder why so many people are feeling burned out, unsettled and lost.

That's why I invite you to take the risk and look at everything at once. Think of it like traversing the wilderness and climbing a tree or hiking to the top of a rise so you can get a more complete picture of the new environment. Then, rather than categorize, we can think about the entire terrain and consider how we might combine or consider things in new ways when operating across domains. Not to drive a quick decision, but to consider different ways when being and doing as an act of sensemaking.

Going back to the puzzle example, you already know how to do this. You try pieces that look like they might fit and try to put them together. When it works, you put them together and grab another piece. When it doesn't, just try another piece or another area of the puzzle. Playing with possibilities *before* we decide raises new questions and offers new possibilities we might not otherwise consider. It also allows us to recalibrate our values or priorities to meet the needs of this What Now? Moment and removes the pressure of making a singular "right" choice in the midst of inquiry. This may mean intentionally putting aside one thing and over-focusing on another—not forever, but for a season. This involves a deeper, more interdimensional look at our work and our lives with a willingness to integrate across domains intentionally rather than waiting to have to do it when the s*&% hits the fan.

We can do this on our own, but there are benefits to collaborating with others. In my research, working together in small groups, in teams, or with a trusted partner can help us to see connections we might not otherwise consider because we are convinced (consciously or unconsciously) that those combinations are impossible for us in our situations. Getting someone with no horse in the race to ask new questions, we can encourage one another to consider new routes, not as advice or an assumption of knowing better, but in the spirit of identifying possibilities, raising new questions, and considering where we might explore further through experimentation.

TAKEAWAYS

- Gathering ideas, thoughts and information across professional and personal domains can help us to make sense of our lives in a holistic way.

- Considering the full locus of possibilities available to us at points of transition can help to identify surprising opportunities, but it takes time, attention and practice.

- Examining all of the information at our disposal and placing everything "on the altar" helps to identify sacred cows and creates space for us to examine our commitments as we discern possible routes forward.

PART THREE

Explore

A note to the reader as you begin to 'Explore'

As we begin to explore, it's helpful to pause and acknowledge all of the learning and work you've done to bring you to this point. You've paused your journey (or at least the forced forward momentum) to develop a better understanding of your relationship with *What Now?* Moments and how your reactions and responses might vary when interruptions or disruptions lead to incendiary emotions, disorientation or stuckness. You've recognized that resilience is more than "I am" or "I'm not" because we are all resilient in some circumstances, and less resilient in others. While identifying your own areas of resilience (or lack thereof) may still feel a bit overwhelming, please know that as you continue to craft a sustainable practice of rigorous self-awareness, you will gain a keener sense of the contours of your own strengths and vulnerabilities. Remember that this is a journey to gather resources for yourself, your family and friends, and your team across emotional, physical, material, social and other variables that are relevant to your unique circumstances.

Hopefully, as you've considered your relationship with change and transition, you've been able to identify one or more metaphors that help to illustrate how you perceive change in this moment. With this in mind, you've asked yourself if your metaphors are helpful or unhelpful, and perhaps have tweaked them or changed them outright. In the spirit of practicing rigorous self-awareness, you've probed questions about who you are, where you are and what might be possible if you gave yourself the time and the space to consider change as a prompt to dispassionate curiosity and a hopeful willingness to consider paths forward that might not seem feasible or available on first blush.

If you're reading this book straight through for the first time, you've likely done more thinking about these things than doing these things. That's okay!

There is a reason this book's subtitle is "learn to" and not "how to." Learning is a process. The goal here is not to solve a particular problem by the end of the book. The goal is to view uncertainty and change as transitional learning space and to embrace the unknown as rich in possibilities when we approach it in new ways. We've teased out some great questions about where we are, what we need, what might be possible over the past several chapters—but that prompts another question: How do we translate the insights (or new questions) we've uncovered into action? One way is to move deeper into inquiry by moving from "ask" to "explore."

But what does that mean in practice? In this section, you're invited to move from gathering and considering questions to finding answers to those questions that can be applied in context.

Press on, explorer!

Joan

CHAPTER EIGHT

Learn by doing

The art and science of experimentation

When I met Jeneanne she was ready for a change. An educator, aspiring designer and single mother of a preteen daughter, she had big aspirations for her small family, and was ready to consider big moves to fulfill them. The particulars were still hazy at the time and involved a number of high-stakes moving parts. This fact and others made her a perfect fit for one of several year-long wayfinding research cohorts I launched that year. Working on her own and with a small group of diverse but like-minded women, her pursuit of rigorous self-awareness, sensemaking and reflection led to some concrete insights, interesting possibilities, and a lot of new questions. She established that she wanted to leave Chicago and that finding an intersection between her expertise as an educator, her love of design, and her deep commitment to social change was a priority. So was her daughter and the deep calling to find a vibrant, culturally enriching community where they both felt valued and nurtured.

When she thought about making a change in practice, however, every option she considered felt monumental—largely because they were. What if she took a job across the country that didn't work out? What if the schools were not a good fit for her daughter? Was it irresponsible to pursue her dreams at the risk of uprooting her child? Was it irresponsible not to? When she considered these questions as prompts for action, it was crystal clear that there was no simple framework or checklist she could follow to answer them. And she didn't want one. An educator and designer at heart, she had a sense of the life she wanted, and the capacity to carry it out. But, in practice, the liminal distance between the Chicago apartment where she and her daughter were living and a new reality living and working on the east coast felt like a chasm. She was ready to move beyond theoretical inquiry and explore how she might shift from identifying possibilities to bringing one of more of them to life, but was not yet ready to make a firm, committed decision. Rather than continue ruminating on "what if?" she engaged in a process of exploring how she might answer these questions in action.

Learning in action

There are many different ways to approach learning about the world around us. This simple fact applies to research scientists developing new theories and individuals as they try to make sense of the day-to-day in practice. In my role as a researcher, I favor ways of knowing that are grounded in learning by doing by co-creating solutions alongside the people who are facing them. That's why I embrace participatory action research (PAR) as a research methodology—and as a way of life. While I won't go deeply into the theory of it here (see Appendix G), the central tenets of action research involve learning about problems by engaging with others to solve them and helping people to strengthen the interconnections between self-awareness, the unconscious, and life in society (Chevalier and Buckles, 2013). Unlike other methods that create distance between the researcher as observer and the research subject as observed, action research allows me to roll up my sleeves and get in the trenches with leaders, teams and individuals and address particular issues, in context, in real time. This can involve many different sorts of interactions, all grounded in learning by doing in community with others. Engagements are designed to shed light on the questions and challenges people face in their own domains and to help them to uncover culturally relevant ways to discover new possibilities that are built by and work for the communities in which they operate. I believe that all of us can benefit from learning to answer the big questions that get us stuck with experimentation.

Let me be clear: in the same way that navigation experts make a distinction between wandering and navigating, when I talk about learning in action, I make a distinction between "trying things" and experimenting. Of course, just like wandering has its place, so does trying things on to see if they fit. I fully support all forms of exploration as instrumental to the creative

In the same way that not all wilderness journeys lend themselves to wandering, some transitions require a more structured approach to exploration.

process and gathering insights that lead (eventually) to deeper learning. But, in the same way that not all wilderness journeys lend themselves to wandering, some transitions require a more structured approach.

This is especially true when resources are in short supply, time is a factor, the stakes are high, and we're stuck in transition. In fact, in my experience with people navigating uncertain transitions, randomly trying things can sometimes contribute to overwhelm and uncertainty. That's why it is critical to remember that, while all experimentation involves exploration, not all exploration is experimentation, and it is important to clarify from the outset which you're are engaged in.

Contrasting Andrea's journey that we discussed previously with Jeneanne's situation provides a helpful illustration of this. In Andrea's case, she made an intentional decision to pack up her life in New York and make space for reflection and wandering with no particular outcome in mind. She chose to invest time and other resources in the opportunity to focus on rigorous self-awareness and replenishment—a sabbatical of sorts guided by some broad questions, but also designed for her to rest and consider possibilities over a longer stretch of time. Her recent move to Stockholm involves more of the same, with an eye on moving from exploration to execution in the coming months. Jeneanne, on the other hand, did not perceive herself to have that luxury.

Both stories are a call to action for organizational leaders—especially in times when an increasingly nomadic talent force seeking to reimagine how they work and live are eager to co-create mutually beneficial solutions to these problems with their employers. There is an opportunity embedded in all of these stories that is worth noting in the context of learning in action. Helping to create space for employees to explore and experiment as they navigate their particular career and life journey is the future of professional and personal development for smart, ambitious and purpose-driven people like Jeneanne, Andrea and others we've discussed. This principle also applies to educators experimenting in the classroom, and healthcare administrators co-creating solutions with their stakeholders. It may seem risky, but creating third spaces for people to explore options and test possibilities without needing to leave—like Ashley's company did for her (Chapter 1)—can have positive results. Unfortunately, not all companies have that kind of mechanism in place for their employees—and most individuals don't create it on their own.

Making space to explore

So, as we think about what it means to move from inquiry into exploration, it is important to acknowledge that what we hope to learn should dictate the way we approach learning it. The best way to learn to build a house is not to read a book, but to work alongside a builder. Psychotherapy or surgery, on the other hand, require some fundamental study of the human mind and body before learning by doing. That's why, when we think about learning by doing, it is not about choosing a right or wrong method of learning but understanding that we can be more creative about what we need to learn and how we want to learn it than simply choosing the latest popular online course or workshop or hoping a Google search that returns 40 million responses will lead us in the right direction.

So where do we begin?

Experiment design canvas

I came to the field of education and research from 17 years of practice in the communications field. Research was always part of that work, but it was predominantly related to very precise questions tied to gathering the particular information the team needed to accomplish a task, a goal or a specific objective. I'd encountered the scientific method in school, of course—but it wasn't until I decided to go to graduate school in my 40s that I learned what academic research was all about. And it was an eye opener! I respect theory building tremendously and publish papers in my field. But, as I mentioned previously, I've always been drawn to the intersection of rigorous inquiry and devoted practice. Through my work with wayfinding and liminal learning, I've come to believe that, in the information-saturated, highly dynamic world we now live in, we are all called upon to be citizen sensemakers and researchers in our own domains.

FIGURE 8.1 Experiment design canvas

EXPERIMENT DESIGN CANVAS

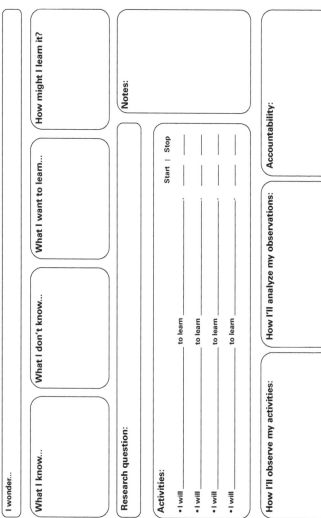

I wonder...

What I know...

What I don't know...

What I want to learn...

How might I learn it?

Notes:

Research question:

Activities:

- I will _____ to learn _____
- I will _____ to learn _____
- I will _____ to learn _____
- I will _____ to learn _____

Start | Stop

How I'll observe my activities:

How I'll analyze my observations:

Accountability:

Yet, since this is an emerging phenomenon, we are not educated, equipped, or even focused on developing these new capacities and skills. Instead, we rely on thought leaders, social media influencers, and friends and family as our wayfinding tools and hope for the best. I created the experiment design canvas (see Figure 8.1) to help people think about experimentation at work or at home beyond throwing noodles on the wall to see if they stick. Instead, you can use this simple framework to develop a more deliberate way of structuring and launching time-boxed exploratory experiments that are designed to answer particular research questions.

Although it has its basis in the scientific method, the canvas is meant to bring some precision to the art of wayfinding when you have questions that you'd like to explore through experimentation. It is important to note that this does not promise quick, easy answers. Instead, like the resilience wheel, the hope compass, the sensemaking spaces and other approaches to inquiry we've discussed, it was created in the field as a tool to help wayfinders put the *learning* in learning by doing in their own ways. Launching experiments as a means to engage with relevant possibilities that emerge from the sensemaking process before making a concrete decision can be a helpful part of an active waiting practice. Experimentation provides a way to take time-boxed actions without committing to a particular course or decision in the long term. Many people find this liberating. For others it is too structured or not intuitive.

I invite you to play with it and see if it is for you. If it isn't, then put it down and move on. Design your own exploration tools that work for you. Better yet, send me a note and we'll design one together! The key here is not to create a massive tribe of experiment design canvas users. Instead, I hope for more people to recognize that, by choice or necessity, we are all increasingly in the wilderness more than we are on the path. As a result, identifying, creating, and playing with sensemaking and wayfinding tools is a fundamental skill for navigating modern life. In the spirit of the tool itself, the best way to know whether or not the experiment design canvas is for you is to experiment with using it. Like any

FIGURE 8.2 I wonder...

EXPERIMENT DESIGN CANVAS

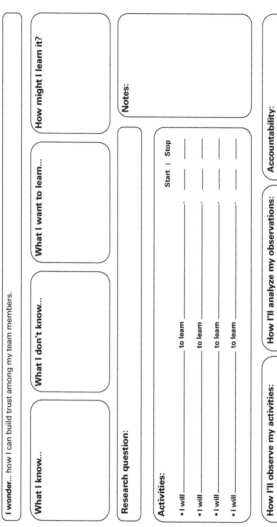

I wonder... how I can build trust among my team members.

What I know...

What I don't know...

What I want to learn...

How might I learn it?

Research question:

Activities:

- I will _____ to learn _____
- I will _____ to learn _____
- I will _____ to learn _____
- I will _____ to learn _____

Start | Stop

Notes:

How I'll observe my activities:

How I'll analyze my observations:

Accountability:

creative act of exploration, you need to develop your own practice. Let's take and example piece by piece to illustrate. In Figure
8.2 I offer a simple but common question that runs through many
of the stories we've encountered in the previous chapters: I wonder
how I can build trust among my team members?

I wonder...

"I wonder" questions are big picture, visionary questions that prompt
consideration of many possibilities rather than a yes, no or maybe. They
can point to who we are (I wonder who I will become if I stay in this
job), where we hope to go (I wonder if I am meant to live in Spain), or
how we hope to live, like in our example. In any case, these questions
prompt secondary questions like: What do you mean by living a life
that matters? What are your dreams? Are you prone to burning out?
What's your time horizon for deciding your life matters? "I wonder"
questions are an invitation to dig deeper and get to the questions behind
the question. They are also the kinds of questions that can spark incendiary emotions when answers feel out of our grasp and we allow them
to shift from creative prompts (I wonder how I might live a life that
matters) to declarative statements (I will never have a life that matters,
or I *know* I will live a life that matters) regardless of evidence in either
direction. By creating a practice of defaulting to wonder, we are more
prone to curiosity and can move naturally into inquiry to understand
what we know, what we don't know, and how we might find out.

From "I wonder" to "let's find out"

Just below the "I wonder" question there are four spaces in the
experiment design canvas that are designed to prompt reflection
on what is and is not known and possible ways of finding out.
This can involve traditional research: reading books, taking
courses, observation. It can also include actions like connecting

FIGURE 8.3   What I do/don't know

EXPERIMENT DESIGN CANVAS

I wonder... how I can build trust among my team members.

What I know...
- There is some infighting on the team
- People are not communicating
- Two people are looking for new jobs

What I don't know...
- The source of the disruption
- What role leadership is playing in the challenge

What I want to learn...
- What action I can take to make positive change
- What I'm doing to contribute to the problem

How might I learn it?
- Connect with team members one on one
- Make space for anonymous feedback
- Create ways to observe team connections

Notes:

Research question:

Activities:

Start | Stop

- I will _____ to learn _____ ___ ___
- I will _____ to learn _____ ___ ___
- I will _____ to learn _____ ___ ___
- I will _____ to learn _____ ___ ___

How I'll observe my activities:

How I'll analyze my observations:

Accountability:

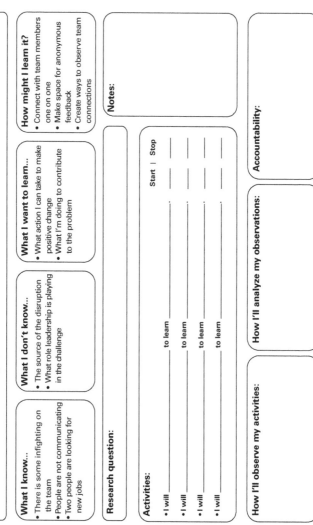

FIGURE 8.4 Research question and activities

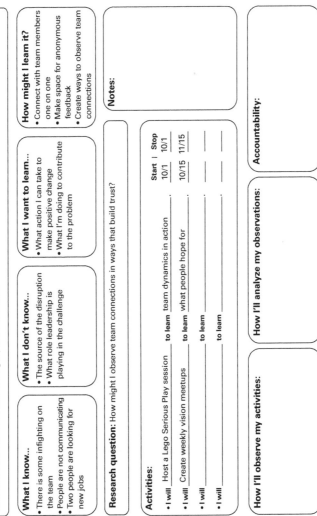

EXPERIMENT DESIGN CANVAS

I wonder... how I can build trust among my team members.

What I know...
- There is some infighting on the team
- People are not communicating
- Two people are looking for new jobs

What I don't know...
- The source of the disruption
- What role leadership is playing in the challenge

What I want to learn...
- What action I can take to make positive change
- What I'm doing to contribute to the problem

How might I learn it?
- Connect with team members one on one
- Make space for anonymous feedback
- Create ways to observe team connections

Research question: How might I observe team connections in ways that build trust?

Activities:

		Start	Stop
• **I will** Host a Lego Serious Play session **to learn** team dynamics in action		10/1	10/1
• **I will** Create weekly vision meetups **to learn** what people hope for		10/15	11/15
• **I will** _____ **to learn** _____		___	___
• **I will** _____ **to learn** _____		___	___

How I'll observe my activities:

How I'll analyze my observations:

Notes:

Accountability:

with people, launching a trial run, or testing a possibility in a low-stakes environment. Be as thorough as possible in this section because what you uncover here will help to identify the specific research question(s) that will guide your experiments. Figure 8.3 illustrates the gap between what the learner in our example knows and does not know in the first two sections and points to several things they want to learn about their "I wonder" question.

Research questions and time-boxed activities

There are at least three research questions that easily flow out of the "what I want to learn" and "how might I learn it" sections in Figure 8.3. The person in our example could choose to explore ways to connect one on one with team members, to make space for anonymous feedback, or to observe team connections. For our purposes, we'll engage with the third option with a set of time-boxed exploratory activities (see Figure 8.4). Creating the experiment with a set time horizon—whether that be three days or three months—is important, because it frees us up to take concrete actions without forcing an immediate decision.

Observations, analysis and accountability

Before you kick off your experiment, it is helpful to think about how you will capture your learning along the way so you can use it to make sense of the experience and gather insights that might inform your next steps. This can involve journaling, keeping voice notes, taking photographs, sending yourself notes or emails. Anything that fits in the rhythm of your day-to-day activities and prompts your thoughts, memories or imagination when the process is complete—including checking in with a partner or a friend. You might also think in advance about how you want to make sense of your observations, because it can help you to decide how to capture them. In our example

FIGURE 8.5 Observations and accountability

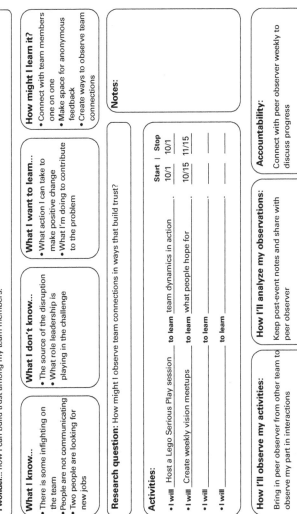

EXPERIMENT DESIGN CANVAS

I wonder... how I can build trust among my team members.

What I know...
- There is some infighting on the team
- People are not communicating
- Two people are looking for new jobs

What I don't know...
- The source of the disruption
- What role leadership is playing in the challenge

What I want to learn...
- What action I can take to make positive change
- What I'm doing to contribute to the problem

How might I learn it?
- Connect with team members one on one
- Make space for anonymous feedback
- Create ways to observe team connections

Notes:

Research question: How might I observe team connections in ways that build trust?

Activities:

				Start	Stop
• I will	Host a Lego Serious Play session	to learn	team dynamics in action	10/1	10/1
• I will	Create weekly vision meetups	to learn	what people hope for	10/15	11/15
• I will		to learn			
• I will		to learn			

How I'll observe my activities:
Bring in peer observer from other team to observe my part in interactions

How I'll analyze my observations:
Keep post-event notes and share with peer observer

Accountability:
Connect with peer observer weekly to discuss progress

(see Figure 8.5), the learner chose to bring in a peer observer as a second set of eyes, and to help the experiment designer to be part of the observation and have an objective view of the process.

Experiments are not decisions

If we choose the experimental approach to learning in action, it is important that we fully embrace the notion that *taking a step* in a certain direction is not a *decision to go* in that direction. This can seem counterintuitive for those of us who were raised in cultures that favor making a decision prior to action—preferably the "right" decision. Instead, by creating these experiments and exploring possible routes forward through action rather than speculation in a structured way, we can answer questions in practice rather than theory. "I don't think I would like coding" becomes "I wonder if I like coding? Perhaps I can code for 45 minutes a day for two months and see what I learn—about coding and about how I feel about coding." By taking steps in one direction or another, we can make sense of unfamiliar terrain and gain deeper understanding of the possibilities and choices in front of us.

This mimics a fascinating tactic that some trained wilderness experts use when they find themselves lost in the woods. First, they mark the spot where they first notice they are lost with a pile of rocks or another marker, so they are firm in their starting place. Then, using string or another marker (many backwoods explorers carry string for this very reason), they walk as far as they can in a direction of their choosing and tie a string on a tree or bush. Then, they walk further and do the same when the string is almost out of sight. They repeat the procedure until they either find a path or a landmark that is a better way forward, or they return to the pile of rocks and repeat the same procedure at 5 or 10 degrees in a different direction. They continue the process of moving out and back again until they've either found their way out or made a complete circle in all directions with the pile of rocks at the center like a giant bicycle wheel with the rocks at the hub and lines of string as the spokes.

As you can imagine, this process will generally result in at least one of three things: 1) they find a way forward, 2) they have a much better understanding of a much larger area of territory so they can make a more educated next step, or 3) they create a much larger and more visible target for anyone who is out there looking for them.

This approach can be extended and translated to experimentation in our own professional and personal lives when we find ourselves at an impasse or point of transition. Taking steps in one direction or another as an experiment and not a decision frees us up to explore without the pressure of deciding which direction we are "meant" to go.

Taking steps in one direction or another as an experiment and not a decision frees us up to explore without the pressure of deciding which direction we are "meant" to go.

When we no longer feel burdened to choose which way to go before we begin, we are freed up to enter a process of exploration, where we are in active inquiry and discernment, rather than choosing a lane. This allows us to either discover a clear path forward or to learn more about ourselves, our circumstances and our options by doing. We can still gather new skills, make the money we need to pay our bills and live well while doing it. We're simply operating in the container of liminal learning—practicing active waiting through experimentation—before we make a firm choice. This approach also opens us up to new people, new experiences and, potentially, new opportunities that we might not have encountered (or had the courage to pursue) had we stayed still or required a firm comittment without first experimenting and gathering additional information.

Figuring it out or sussing it out

Language can be very helpful (or unhelpful) as we attempt to move from viewing uncertain transitions as a problem to solve to a more exploratory engagement with not knowing and an uncertain path forward. The phrase to "figure it out" is familiar to many of us and means *to solve*. It comes from mathematics and frames a problem as having right (or wrong) answer or solution. In uncertain transitions, the right or wrong binary is rarely the case, which can make "figuring it out" an unhelpful prompt for exploring uncharted territory. That's why I prefer to use a less frequently used phrase, to "suss it out." Many people who are familiar with both words view them as synonymous. But, to suss something out means *to discover*. Experimentation means suspending our impulse to figure it out and to approach the process of inquiry in the spirit of discovery. Rather than seek the most efficient solution in the shortest time possible (figure) we make time to ask great questions and seek surprising possibilities. Suss it out.

Experiment in practice

In Jeneanne's case, she knew that Chicago was no longer serving her needs, and Boston was calling her, despite not having lived there. She was looking to make a career change and believed there might be more opportunity for her on the East Coast. But she also knew there were some personal responsibilities and commitments that might make it difficult for her to make a big move—she had her daughter and her education, friends and wellbeing to think about. Much of it felt insurmountable, which led to stuckness. We discussed the possibility of setting up some low-fidelity experiments to see how she might learn by doing.

This led to two trips to Boston where she and her daughter explored what it might feel like to live in the neighborhood where they were considering moving. During that time, they visited the local schools, connected with the school administrators, and her daughter spent a day there to see how she liked it. She attended local events and made some friends. Spending time in a place you're considering moving to probably doesn't seem like anything surprising or special. It wasn't *what* she did that was different; it was *how* she did it. Rather than trying it out, Jeneanne created small, time-boxed experiments that were designed to answer specific questions and used what she learned across these experiences to guide her way.

Instead of wondering if she would be able to get a job in Boston, could she create a portfolio and apply to jobs in Boston even before she decided to move there? In terms of her daughter, spending two weeks in Boston might answer some questions, but by delineating which questions she wanted to learn more about (How will my daughter feel in the school? How will I feel socially here? What is it like to date here?) she was able to do more than just take a vacation. She attended community events, had a few dates despite knowing she was only in town for two weeks, and arranged for her daughter to spend time in school. All of this provided a better snapshot of what the move would be in practice rather than speculation. It gave her concrete experiences and memories that she and her daughter could discuss in order to understand if this was potentially a right move for them. Two trips to Boston, a new portfolio and a new job later, Jeneanne moved to Boston with a new position—well-informed by action rather than speculation. Experience rather than projection. This is the heart of actively shifting from fear to curiosity rather than simply talking about it.

Of course, the story did not end there. After several months in Boston, yet another opportunity opened up for Jeneanne. She used the same process to consider that What Now? Moment, which she might not have considered otherwise, having just made a big change only months before. But she and her daughter now had an approach to think about the potential for this unexpected change and a language to use to discuss it. They are now in the Pacific Northwest and Jeneanne is in a PhD program, thrilled to be solidifying her career change in this way.

The interesting part about this approach is that heading to Boston or even getting the PhD is not a concrete decision to make a career of it. On the contrary, it was an invitation to explore and gather additional information. This framing made entering new and unfamiliar territory an adventure—one that she is still on years later. When I asked her recently about her choices, she told me there are some elements of where she is and what she is doing that she likes better than others. For now, she is executing on the graduate degree and then will continue exploring when graduation poses the next What Now? Moment.

TAKEAWAYS

- Developing low-stakes, time-boxed experiments can help bring dispassionate curiosity into action as a means for developing a deeper understanding of options to help inform decisions.

- Identifying and testing multiple potential paths forward can help uncover next steps based upon experience rather than conjecture.

- Suspending our impulse to figure things out and making space for discovery before we make firm decisions can remove pressure to choose while opening space for new opportunities and insights to emerge.

CHAPTER NINE

Now pivot!

From exploration to execution

I know, I know. I said in Chapter 3 that we don't want to pivot. That opening a space for active waiting and a time horizon for inquiry and exploration is a fruitful way to move beyond being stuck in the pressure of making a premature decision when we are feeling threatened and lacking clarity about where we are and where we hope to go. And I meant it. When we face a What Now? Moment and cross the threshold into uncharted territory, the pivot metaphor can keep us from pausing to make sense of new terrain and identify the possibilities available to us if we make space to identify and coalesce them around our needs, wants, values and contextual cues. But, although some people are wanderers at heart, ambitions and the reality of day-to-day life mean eventually leaving base camp and heading up (or down) the mountain.

As a practical matter, most of us spend our time moving ourselves, our teams and our organizations between periods of execution to exploration and back again. In the same way that stopping when we face a What Now? Moment and slowing the pace when we are executing to open space for inquiry can feel counterintuitive, it can be surprisingly difficult to make the transition from liminal space back into the world of timelines, plans and concrete decisions after we've made space for exploration.

This is not surprising for people who find their default in exploration. Artists, musicians and other creators sometimes feel like they are at their best when they are creating in a space without structure or boundaries. Liminal space is their sweet spot, since they can explore and experiment with new methods and approaches to their work. This kind of creativity is supercharged in the liminal—as long as it is pointed to creating a piece of art. Unfortunately, many of those same people find it difficult to apply that same creative thinking to business strategy or innovation outside of their creative domain.

Music artist, entrepreneur and tech innovator, Vérité, and her manager and business partner Vanessa Magos are the exceptions to this rule. Before I go too deeply into this example, it is important to mention that Vérité is my daughter, but she and Vanessa take their place among the wayfinders in this book for far more relevant reasons than her relationship to me. The two of them have spent the past seven years reimagining how music is created, distributed, valued and shared outside of traditional paths like music labels. From funding their project like a startup through angel investing, to engaging with cutting-edge music makers through podcasts, to experimenting with the blockchain, Vérité and Magos have mastered the art of moving from exploration to execution and back again as a way to carve a new way forward in an industry driven by well-worn pathways.

"This project was born in a What Now? Moment," Vérité told me, referring to a contract with a major label that fell through at the last minute. "It hadn't occurred to us to go independent at the time, but necessity inspired new questions about how music gets made and what resources we needed to make a quality album." That reflection switched the inquiry from "How do I get signed to a label?" to "How can we access the funds we need to produce a quality album without one?" "That's when my identity shifted from music artist to creative entrepreneur. We've been experimenting and pivoting ever since."

Wait, I thought you said don't pivot

We've acknowledged that moving from the forward motion of a journey metaphor to creating a container for exploration territory can prove difficult given the cultural pressure to constantly move forward. What Now? Moments that disrupt or interrupt our journey provide us with the impetus to stop, engage in inquiry, and explore new options. But leaving the liminal container we created and returning to the journey, if that is the intention, is its own What Now? Moment that invites us to pivot from *exploration* to *execution*.

In Chapter 3, we challenged the pivot metaphor as unhelpful when a What Now? Moment invites us to slow the momentum, question perpetual motion, and allow ourselves to enter a transitional learning space. But how much learning is enough? What does it take to move from *divergent thinking*, which is what we're doing when we *explore many possible solutions in order to make new connections* to *convergent thinking*, which involves *organizing ideas in order to arrive at a particular choice* (Razumnikova, 2013)?

There are many models in design and other fields that discuss the importance of divergent and convergent thinking, but few of them talk about what it takes to move from one to the other. At what point have we learned what we need to learn from the experiment? How muddy do things have to be in order for us to characterize them as a What Now? Moment? How do we know when and how to pivot from wayfinding to waymaking?

Moving from wayfinding to waymaking

If you haven't gotten the memo yet, I am all about exploring, experimenting and learning. I have come to believe that it is a key part of working and living in liminal times. Opening up space to make sense of What Now? Moments and navigate through uncertainty is imperative—but at some point we can find ourselves with the desire (or the necessity) to choose a particular path forward or risk getting as stuck in exploration as we are in constant execution. So, how do we get out of base camp and back on the mountain? Asked another way, what does it take to discern between the locus of possibilities we've identified in our sensemaking activities and taking concrete steps forward—even small ones—while acknowledging that we don't know what will happen when we do?

Discernment at points of inflection

Figure 9.1 illustrates the experience of moving between exploration and execution and back again. By now you should be clear on how What Now? Moments catalyze inquiry and execution, but discerning between options and choosing how to press forward after we've gathered information and done our best to make sense is both an art and a science. A science because there are times that our inquiry and exploration lead to precise answers and firm decisions, like they would if someone lost in the woods climbed a tree to get a better view and saw a road close by. An art because sometimes we try multiple things, learn from them, and want or need to move forward, but have yet to identify a firm direction. This can be another kind of What Now? Moment that sparks a different sort of inquiry—the movement from divergent thinking to convergent thinking.

FIGURE 9.1 Discernment framework

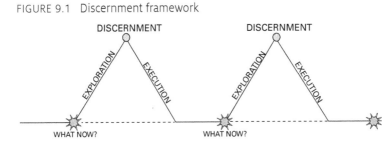

Just like the What Now? Moments that spark exploration, a What Now? Moment at a point of discernment can be viewed in the same way, just in a different direction. Rather than *stop, ask, and explore* how to open up liminal learning space, we can apply the same principles to learning how best to leave the liminal and pursue a course of action. This does not involve a set of particular steps—it is an approach. A set of practices. A way of being in the world that allows us to be interrupted and disrupted and constantly learning, discerning and choosing new ways forward—but always with an eye on interrogating those decisions to confirm that we are headed into the next leg of the journey in a direction that makes sense given what we've learned and is aligned with our aspirations, values and beliefs.

Sensemaking, discernment and moving into execution

In a perfect world, we would conduct our exploration and a single, well-lit, smooth and obvious path would open up ahead of us. And sometimes it does. Sometimes we get the call from our dream job, or the way is perfectly clear ahead of us. Unfortunately, sometimes the What Now? Moment out of inquiry is its own inquiry. Take the case of Erin Rech.

"Thank you so much for picking up the phone!"

Erin Rech, a high-energy communications executive I'd been working with for months, was knee deep in a job change and the process was down to two desirable executive positions. She needed to give an answer that afternoon and she found herself at an impasse. "The money and title are the same," she told me. "Same city and equal prestige." She went through a few other typical variables and was convinced that there was no difference between the two positions. By the time we connected, she just short of flipping a coin.

Erin had spent the previous several months developing a wayfinding practice driven by dispassionate curiosity, inquiry and experimentation. This contributed to her decision to leave her current role and transition to one that would give her the time and space she needed to concentrate on a book project that she was very passionate about. Shifting jobs would also be instrumental in her gathering the resources she would need to explore some other things that had the potential to change her professional and personal trajectory in profound ways. Erin was more than capable of making this decision without my input but had grown accustomed to opening up space for dispassionate curiosity and inquiry when she found herself at a point of uncertain transition. As a result, she wasn't looking for my advice. Instead, she was practicing active resilience by asking if I knew of any wayfinding tools that might help her to distinguish between two equally desirable paths forward. She'd done the work, and now needed to pivot from wayfinding to waymaking.

Thus, if stop, ask, explore *is the process of finding our way into and through uncharted territory,* learn, discern, choose, confirm *is the threshold to make our way out.*

When we think about making sense of where we've been after we've explored through inquiry and experimentation, we can begin the process of moving out of uncharted territory into a new path of our choosing. This may be an existing path that we choose to follow—like taking one of the jobs Erin had at her disposal. Or it can be trying something completely new. Whatever the choice, moving out of exploration is a form of What Now? Moment that is informed by the information and experiences gleaned in the wilderness. Thus, if *stop, ask, explore* is the threshold to finding our way into and through uncharted territory, *learn, discern, choose, confirm* is the threshold to make our way out (see Figure 9.2).

Learn

By the time we consider moving from exploration to execution, we've learned a thing or two about what we like, what we don't like, what we value. We've also done some thinking about who we are and where we might hope to go—even if we haven't landed squarely on a precise destination. So, we've explored and experimented, which is great. But what did we learn from all of it? Just as we stopped at the beginning of this journey into uncharted territory, we also need to stop (briefly) on our way out. Without this pause, we might view things too simply or, once we hit the point of executing again, we may forget what we learned in the same way we do a few weeks after a motivational retreat or other reflective event. What we want to do here is

FIGURE 9.2 Learn, discern, choose, confirm

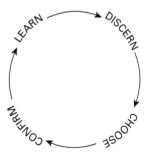

return to where we started. It's a time to pull out those Miro boards, Post-it notes and consider how we marked our entrance into the liminal learning space to really recall who we were and what direction we were headed in before and during our What Now? Moment. Go back to that X you created to mark the spot of entry into liminal space when you decided to enter inquiry and explore new possibilities. Then intentionally compare and contrast our perspectives on where we are now and where we started so we can identify what we've learned, how we've changed and our sense of direction.

QUESTIONS FOR REFLECTION

What insights have you gathered from your exploration so far?

What new questions have bubbled up?

What resistance is coming against you as you move from exploration to executing on your new knowledge?

What excited you about what you've learned?

What sparks fear or frustration?

Discern

Now, taking what we've learned, we can return to the locus of possibilities (Chapter 7) and see how they do or do not fit together. Do they remain distinct and separate items? Are there some that have morphed? Did what we took away from experimentation shift anything or point us to one or the other that becomes a clearer priority? Do we have new questions that need answering before we move forward, or can we begin to move toward a clearer path? These questions prompt reflection so we can more easily determine if we've gathered the information and insights we need to make sense of what we've uncovered (remember those puzzle pieces?) and discern how to proceed from here. Zoom out to collect thoughts and insights across all of the different domains to explore how the relative variables work together as a system.

Choose

In some cases, one choice will easily win out over the others. In others, as in Erin's situation, no clear choice will emerge. There are many ways to break a tie in this sort of situation. You can flip a coin, or you can resort to children's games like rock, paper, scissors. But these are effectively guessing games, and if you've taken the time to explore deeply what is possible, the decisions may come more easily. There are so many resources out there to help with choice making. In fact, as mentioned earlier, it is what most of our existing tools are designed to support. In Erin's case, she had considered her positions based upon typical variables: money, prestige, benefits. To break the tie, I invited her to consider some different domains, drawn from research my colleagues and I conducted to understand customer delight (Parasuraman et al, 2020) This exercise helped her to break the tie and see a clear distinction between two positions through the lens of six less common variables, all of which have been determined to drive delight.

EXERCISE

Designing for delight

Making sense of insights and information across domains invites us to consider what we need, want and value. The following items have been shown, individually and combined, to drive delight. Designing for delight involves considering these delight variables in addition to more concrete and specific factors like money, fame and happiness. It also makes space for delight to emerge in one domain when it is lacking in another.

1 Emotions

While what makes us happy is often used as an orientation tool, we know that it is a fleeting emotion that can be affected by uncertainty and exploring the unknown. There are a range of other positive emotions that can be more enduring in times of change and beyond such as contentment, gratitude, joy and peace that can be used instead of or in addition to happiness as a point of discernment. Consider how your locus of possibilities influences positive and negative emotions.

2 People

Our relationships with others and the communities in which we live and work are critically important to us as routes to delight. The aspects of who we will work with—or how work will affect our relationships outside of work—can be a useful tool to differentiate between options or to inform how we frame possibilities.

3 Getting the job done

This relates to goal setting. What problems do we want to solve for ourselves and others? What do we aspire to or hope for? Fulfilling our aspirations can be delightful and making choices that allow us to pursue a meaningful path can be crucial to wellbeing and flourishing. This might be a good time to return to the hope compass.

4 Beauty and environment

This refers to our environment and surroundings. It can relate to our office space or our homes. Aesthetics and beauty. How and where we are inspired in our spaces and places. Is it high on your list of needs or is living or working in uninspiring space a limiting factor for you? These questions can be helpful for discernment.

5 Timing
The timing of things being in alignment with our needs and expectations can be a source of delight or frustration. If we hope for things to move quickly, but others move slowly, that can cause distress. The opposite can be true when we want to take our time and feel rushed. Is the timing you're working with in alignment with your expectations and hopes? Do you have the flexibility to make things happen?

6 Freedom
The level of control or influence we have on outcomes and how we approach experiences and circumstances is another important variable. Do you prefer structured environments where you are given set tasks and timetables? If so, too much freedom to pave your own way might be unsettling. If you like having the freedom to schedule your activities, as long as the job gets done, too much structure can feel limiting. How much structure makes sense for you? What level of agency inspires you?

Allowing yourself to explore what's next based upon what will create delight for you and for those you hope to serve can be a useful tool for sensemaking and discernment.

Confirm

Moving forward from here — or on any journey— it is a good idea to create your own system or framework to help determine if the path you're on is one you actually want to be on. That confirmation can be based on a timetable, outcomes or on something else. The particulars are less important than committing to a practice of carrying forward into the execution all that you have learned in order to help to confirm whether you've chosen a path that makes sense to you or, if not, that you identify that quickly and acknowledge that you are facing another What Now? Moment. There is nothing wrong with this, of course, since all times of execution will eventually lead to another What Now? Moment. The key is to bring humility into our choices so we are able to recognize that we might have chosen poorly and that we should not persist if the evidence uncovers that we' re moving in the wrong direction.

Execution to exploration and back again

The process of moving from execution to exploration and back again is the ebbing and flowing of life that we've all experienced, but we rarely consider the day-to-day. This is not about embracing a new process any more than naming and acknowledging the differences between spring, summer, winter and fall is. Instead, it is about acknowledging that our sense of (or lack of) clarity about our sense of direction waxes and wanes like the tides or the phases of the moon. We can survive perfectly well without identifying and acknowledging that—but it can also be helpful to see it for what it is and develop our own approaches to moving between them. If we do, it can help us to locate ourselves in both times of execution and times of exploration. It will provide us with the insight we need to access the right resources at the right time to navigate the part of the trail we find ourselves on and to have a better shot at finding and making our way through uncharted territory and back again.

TAKEAWAYS

- The move from wayfinding to waymaking is its own What Now? Moment.
- The transition from divergent and convergent thinking involves sensemaking and discernment.
- We can see where we are in this transition by understanding where we are on the *learn, discern, choose, confirm* spectrum.

CHAPTER TEN

Now follow your passion!

"I'm not a hero or a role model," Evan Dittig told me, "I'm just a skateboarder who loves it so much that I want to share that passion through education, service to others, here and across the globe." Evan is the founder and executive director of Shred.Co, an education company whose stated mission is to improve mental, physical, and social wellbeing on a local and global scale through skateboarding. A sponsored skateboarder since he was in his teens, Evan believes skateboarding can be a force for good, not just in his community, but around the world. In addition to running programs for children (and their parents!), he conducts therapeutic skateboarding engagements for mentally handi-capped and addicted adults in the United States and is part of a global network of skateboard educators representing every continent who are committed to the sport as a means to build skills, capacity and confidence.

"The sickest part is that I'm actually able to make a living and support myself and my lifestyle just through skateboarding and sharing my passion and what I love to do with others, which is the coolest thing." By applying the principles we've discussed in the previous chapters, Evan was able to identify a way to braid his love of skateboarding, his desire to be an educator/entrepreneur, and a deep desire to help others into a single entity that is as much a calling as a business. "Hopefully these kids will be doing awesome things when they grow up. That they are inspired to do even better work than I'm doing one day. We'll just all save the world through skateboarding."

This notion may sound strange or narrow to someone who does not share Evan's passion for his sport, but that is irrelevant. His trips to South Africa, Cuba and Nicaragua, and equipment drives to send new boards and skate shoes to young people in Zambia, Angola, Zimbabwe, Mozambique and South Africa are a testament to his drive and commitment. Born from passion, his initiative speaks for itself.

Yes, I said passion.

In the same way that the last chapter returned us to the concept of the pivot, we return to our passions and how they can motivate us to move from exploration to execution and persevere when we face resistance. As with the other practices we've explored together, I invite you to focus less on whether it is right or wrong to pivot or not pivot or follow your dispassion or passion, and think about liminal space as space we learn to move in and out of routinely. Passion, pivots, convergent and divergent thinking are all practices that are available to us and potentially helpful, if applied in ways that are appropriate to the situation and contexts in which we find ourselves. Following our passions when we are caught up in incendiary emotions—positive or negative—can create noise in the system, and drive us to make decisions that don't take into consideration all of the variables that might help us explore the entire locus of possibilities at our disposal when we face an uncertain transition. But, as we move out of exploration and into execution—from wayfinding to waymaking, as we discussed in Chapter 9—the very dispassion that helped us to pause and move into inquiry and exploration can be a barrier to the motivation, perseverance and grit we need to stay the course and execute on our ideas and ambitions.

The key takeaway here is that we do not employ wayfinding practices to return to business as usual—even if the entire process results in recommitting to the course we were on before. The act of reorienting ourselves and engaging in liminal learning is meant to help us to reinvigorate, or identify for the first time, what matters to us and how we can engage our passions as a source of motivation. It's not just a matter of determining what *direction* I should go, but what it is that *motivates* me to go there? Both elements influence the bigger question we've been exploring here—how to get unstuck.

The very dispassion that helped us pause and move into inquiry and exploration can be a barrier to the motivation, perseverance and grit we need to stay the course and execute on our ideas and ambitions.

How much is enough?

This brings us back around to some of the challenges that get many people stuck in the first place—a lack of clarity about what they are passionate about and how to bring those passions to life in a way that is sustainable. The value of wayfinding is that, rather than finding ourselves stuck because we don't have an answer to these larger questions, we now have practices, principles and approaches we can draw upon to uncover what we find meaningful, and explore the varied routes we might take to get there, perhaps over a longer time horizon than we'd originally planned. Stuckness becomes an invitation to pause, ask new questions and explore, rather than view uncertainty as a threat.

This allows us to view following our passions as less of an incendiary response to an urgent call to win a race we may or may not have chosen to run, and more as a creative prompt that inspires us to reflect on who we are and what matters to us—and to others. This is what Evan did as he reflected on what inspires him, and where his passions intersect with the impact he hopes to make. His efforts are both global and local by design—a networked structure that is small enough to let him engage with the individuals he serves at an intimate level. He does not seek to serve tens of millions, but to work at the grassroots level across the globe. This global/local approach is aligned with the spirit of skateboarding culture and brings him great joy. This level of impact has given him a sense of personal and professional alignment at a scale that is both manageable and sustainable.

Stuckness becomes an invitation to pause, ask new questions and explore, rather than view uncertainty as a threat.

Pursuing your passions and making an impact

In a world where scale is favored, grassroots efforts like Evan's are sometimes perceived as less important than massive efforts that reach millions of people. Greater scale, more important, the thinking might go. And at some level, that makes sense. When it comes to deploying a vaccine for Covid-19 or developing a cure for cancer, scale is key. Like so many other things in this book, I take a both/and view on the matter of scale. There are many worthwhile things that are good for individuals and communities that happen at scale. That said, how or if we scale is an essential wayfinding question that we often overlook.

I cannot tell you how many times I've sat across a table or on the other side of a video call with someone whose What Now? Moment involves a decision about growing, changing, or something else related to bigger and more. I love that, and am happy to help people reach really high-end goals at senior levels. I work with executives, thought leaders, and people who are trying to make big changes in ways that will have world-scale impact. Fantastic.

But that's not everyone.

We looked at the hope compass in Chapter 6 and considered the big questions: What do we hope for? What problems do we hope to solve? Whose problems? Why are we the right ones to solve them? What are the many possible ways we might solve them? What we didn't discuss is at what scale we should solve them—or the fact that the same aspiration can be deployed at many different levels of scale and still be profoundly meaningful. Unfortunately, we sometimes lose sight of this when we move fast and pivot forward without making time to consider if more, or bigger, or faster is always better. Let's think about this using a much-discussed current example: lifelong learning and skill building.

It is no secret that keeping our skills current and engaging in lifelong learning is a challenge we all face living in a rapidly changing world. Whether the focus is on equipping young people to be prepared for careers that don't yet exist, cross-training displaced mid-career workers for tech careers, or training emerging and established leaders to develop and employ new models to support the needs of a hybrid workforce, lifelong learning and helping people to equip themselves for the future is a fundamental challenge we face in the 2020s and beyond.

If we were to pose the question to a random room full of people in the education and learning sector across the globe, I am confident we would receive wildly different ideas about how best to address these very real challenges. One person (or more likely a large team) might suggest creating an online platform that can be accessed worldwide and provides a culturally relevant curriculum in multiple languages tied in with local offerings in ways that support what is happening on the ground. This sort of a project would necessitate global interaction and raising millions of dollars to create the necessary infrastructure. If the leaders pull it off, they might reach millions of people and wind up on a 30 under 30 or 50 over 50 list and their efforts will garner press coverage. A large part of the day-to-day work for someone running an organization at that scale is executive-level oversight, relationship building, and gathering and connecting resources in support of a vision that goes way further than one community or neighborhood. This is the sort of grand vision many people have in mind (consciously or unconsciously) when they think about making a difference or doing something that has purpose or meaning. The people who set out to do these things and actually make it are the ones we view as successful. We look up to them and aspire to be them. They take a global view of life and address the systems and intersections we face across and between borders.

And we need them!

FIGURE 10.1 Impact funnel

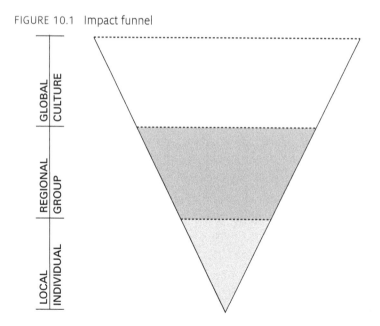

But there are millions upon millions of people who are operating at other levels of attention in the education and learning domain. In fact, the vast majority of us have impact that is closer to the ground and less oriented toward solving global problems at scale. That's why understanding what level of impact we want to have, and at what scale, can both inform our wayfinding and help us to view our efforts at any scale as valuable and worthwhile, whether or not they will land us on a list in *Forbes* or *Fortune*. The impact funnel in Figure 10.1 provides a helpful visual reference for bringing our hopes for ourselves and others to life at whatever level of engagement makes sense to us.

Hope and impact

As we consider the prompt of the impact funnel, it is helpful to remember the hope compass, since these tools can work very well together. As you ask what problem you want to solve and whose problem you hope to solve, you can get a deeper understanding of your intentions if you also ask, where are those people? How many are there? Are they in my community or are they elsewhere? In doing so, you may uncover new opportunities—or give yourself a chance to rethink what particular impact you hope to have. In Evan's case, his hope is to bring confidence, connection and community to the people he serves, and it is at the center of all that he does. This passion can become a light that will help him to discern the shape Shred.Co will take over the coming years—and the impact it will have in doing so. If Evan expands beyond his passion for being on the skate board, connecting with other skaters, or creating community, he may build a bigger business, but not one that holds the same meaning to him or those he serves. If he remains smaller and more nimble, he may not spread worldwide. Neither path is better or worse than the other. Impact has many shapes and sizes. And needs exist at every level of engagement. Does a person who devotes their life to caring for a single disabled child have a lesser impact than one who builds a global network?

That depends upon what you hope for, what problem you hope to solve, whose problem you want to solve, and how you want to solve it.

TAKEAWAYS

- A passionate response to moving from exploration to execution can motivate action and intention.

- Understanding where our passions help and where they hinder our wayfinding journey can help us to determine when to follow them and when they might lead us astray.

- The scale at which we choose to bring our passions to life can help to orient us on our wayfinding journey.

CHAPTER ELEVEN

What Now? Moments and life in uncharted territory

It is time now to explore the creative potential of interrupted and conflicted lives, where energies are not narrowly focused or permanently pointed toward a single ambition. These are not lives without commitments but lives in which commitments are continually refocused and redefined.

MARY CATHERINE BATESON

The uncertain transitions we face across the span of our interrupted and conflicted lives offer tremendous creative potential to reflect, refocus and redefine our commitments.

JOAN BALL

"It's strange," Sarah said, looking up from her camera to find the words as I watched across Zoom. "I know things are completely screwed up, but I feel surprisingly calm." It was mid-March 2020, and we were chatting about her response to the Covid-19 pandemic at work and in her personal life. I'd been working with Sarah for about six months before the lockdown as part of a work-based training program. We hadn't spoken for two months before the pandemic hit, but she'd recognized it as a What Now? Moment, mapped some metaphors, and was curiously considering how she might experiment her way through an unprecedented time in modern history. "I still don't know exactly what to do next," she told me. "But I feel lighter. Like I know I this is uncharted territory, and I will find a way through."

I received many similar calls from people in early 2020. People who were adjusting more quickly and getting their bearings more easily because they had begun to understand their relationship with uncertainty and were developing their own unique practices with regard to a global What Now? Moment that led to so many different interruptions and disruptions for people in so many contexts. I spoke to leaders who were wrestling with what to do for their teams at the same time as determining what to do with, and for, their kids' education. I spoke to frontline workers sussing out ways to see their and families without exposing them to the virus. I spoke to hundreds of students navigating transitions at school and into the workforce. A grand and ubiquitous What Now? Moment experienced in so many particular ways by as many particular people.

As I've underscored in the preceding pages, these people were not pulling out a checklist and following a prescribed process. And thank goodness for that. Had that been the case, it is highly unlikely that anything I or anyone else might have suggested would have been relevant to so many people dealing with such different circumstances. Instead, by bringing the wayfinding principles they'd created for themselves to bear on their unique circumstances within the larger challenge, they were able to recognize their threat response and gather the resources they needed to have the best chance to respond rather than react.

While Covid-19 is a historic What Now? Moment, it confirmed how critical it is for us to prepare ourselves for the unimaginable by developing frameworks and approaches and built on a foundation of self-awareness and a recognition that understanding who we are and where we hope to go is an evolving practice that unfolds across a lifetime. Keeping ourselves oriented and reoriented as we face what life brings is an invitation to dispassionate curiosity, inquiry and exploration, which requires attention, patience and humility, especially since we humans are prone to walk in circles.

Walking in circles

In his book *Finding Your Way Without a Map or a Compass* (1999), Harold Gatty describes why people tend to walk in circles—whether or not they are lost. His observations, which are based on research in a variety of contexts and with different communities of people across the globe, offer some insight into why navigation can be so challenging, regardless of our wayfinding skills and practices.

The challenge starts with who we are and how we're structured. Our right- or left-handedness creates strength differentials that impact direction in rowing, swimming or walking. Even a minimum difference in leg length can influence our direction over miles. "Practically everybody deviates," Gatty states. "Among the majority of people, the full blindfold deviation circle is formed in about half an hour. Others become displaced more slowly and may take from one to six hours to complete a circle. Practically nobody continues in a straight line." The degree of error is so consistent that he recommends that field training involve measuring the direction and extent of the general deviation so it can be accounted for when navigating without a map or compass. Dominance of one eye over the other, carrying a pack or even a rope in one hand can also have an impact in ways that are imperceptible in the moment but lead to walking off course and, eventually, in a circle. It's almost like we humans are not built to follow linear paths.

Our environment also influences our path when we, by choice or instinct, veer away from what Gatty calls an "irritant direction." Whether it is wind, rain, dust storms, or even sunshine, the conditions in the spaces we are trying to navigate can cause a person to lean their head away, which impacts direction. Even when a person takes on an irritant force head on, we carry, according to Gatty, a psychological preference to turn one way, usually right, when we face a barrier or a choice. So, he concludes, no matter our approach to navigating without a map or compass, we are being influenced by our physical bodies, our psychological predispositions, the territory in which we find ourselves, and the irritant forces we encounter along the way. Sounds a lot like finding our self-world fit.

Applying this lens to navigating change in uncertain times supports the notion that we wrestle with strengths, limitations, and the rhythms of our minds and bodies—and the "irritant forces" we encounter when changing environments can throw us off course. Perhaps we can learn to travel without walking in circles if we gather the emotional, physical, material, and social resources we toggle between in times of execution and exploration. Or, maybe, we accept that the world of work, life, community, and the systems they exist within might be more suited to our imperfections and peccadillos if they were designed to be less linear and more organic. Perhaps, as we explore what it means to develop a wayfinding mindset and practice our wayfinding skills, we can adapt our expectations to the very real fact that we are built to walk in circles—and the winds of change will not always be at our back. So, as you embark on your own journey, I leave you with the following thoughts and questions to ponder as we come to a close.

No matter our approach to navigating without a map or compass, we are being influenced by our physical bodies, our psychological predispositions, the territory in which we find ourselves, and the irritant forces we encounter along the way. Sounds a lot like finding our self-world fit.

What Now? Moments are inevitable—so prepare

We cannot prevent What Now? Moments from happening. In fact, if we become too obsessed with avoiding What Now? Moments, we can miss the creative opportunities that exist when we find ourselves at the edge of our understanding and comfort. So, as you consider who you are and where you hope to go, now is a good time to reflect:

How do I react to What Now? Moments in general?

Are those reactions different across different territories (home, work, community)?

Are those reactions different across different domains of the resilience wheel?

Are there certain people/circumstances that spark incendiary reactions, responses and behaviors in me and are they helpful or unhelpful?

Under what circumstances do I feel most resilient?

Under what circumstances do I feel least resilient?

When was the last time I reacted disproportionately to a What Now? Moment (i.e. treated it as life and death but later realized it was less incendiary than I thought)?

What is a way I might have dealt with that situation differently had I employed the *stop, ask, explore* framework?

Is there a time when I wish I had taken longer to reflect/consider the scenario and my options more carefully at a point of transition before responding/reacting?

If I had approached the situation dispassionately, might I have responded differently? Would the outcome have been different?

What resources might I gather now to be better prepared for my next What Now? Moment?

How can I help others or people in my team to navigate What Now? Moments?

What are some other questions I should be asking myself now?

Every What Now? Moment is novel—and similar

When a What Now? Moment hits and we are unsure what to do next, the brain responds—no matter how much training we give it. If the change feels like a threat, it can spark our incendiary emotions. Remember, there is nothing wrong with incendiary emotions. We need the full range of emotions in our repertoire. No judgement for emotions, reactions and responses—just proper resourcing to help us learn to regulate and learn from them in ways that are helpful given our context. Some useful questions to reflect on here are:

Under what circumstances do I find it hard to *stop, ask or explore?*

What Now? Moments have I faced over the past five years? Did I fight? Flee? Freeze? Other?

How might I be more aware of future responses so I can detect patterns?

When I detect a negative pattern, what practice can I put into place to help me change my responses when I notice that the pattern may be surfacing?

Who can I ask to observe my behavior and give me honest (and kind!) feedback?

Approaching uncertainty takes confidence and humility

The firefighting metaphor we began with works so well here. Highly trained emergency services personnel bring all of that experience and training to the scene of a fire or other emergency but recognize that, while they know how to fight fires, they do not necessarily know how to fight THIS fire without gathering the best information they can and the appropriate resources they need to respond. This means building skills and developing practices that give us the confidence we need to enter into liminal learning space, but also the humility to accept that we don't know how best to proceed unless we ask questions and are willing to learn from the answers. Here are some questions to reflect upon:

What is my relationship with confidence—and do I need to have more or less of it to be right-sized?

What is my relationship with humility—and do I need to have more or less of it to be right-sized?

Where does my confidence meet humility? How do they intersect?

Would my best friend agree with this assessment?

Would my partner agree?

Would my boss or business partner agree?

Would my subordinates agree?

Wayfinding is an art—no one size fits all

In the same way that any explorer has both tools of the trade and the art of their own approach, wayfinding is about developing new capacities and practicing them in context. Not only will the tools you choose be different than those someone else chooses, but you will also likely have to adapt the tools you use to changing situations and circumstances. That is why this is about embracing a practice rather than implementing a preset framework or set of rules:

Which of the wayfinding practices presented here appeals to me instinctually?

Which of my existing practices might I adapt for wayfinding?

Do these tools suit me in practice as much as they do in theory? If I'm not sure yet, how might I find out?

How might I develop/fine-tune/tweak them further to better suit my own unique personality and needs?

How do I know if I am in a practice of execution (trekking up the mountain)?

How do I know if I am in a practice of exploration (active waiting in base camp)?

How can I practice moving from one to the other more easily?

Helping others to face What Now? Moments?

Learning to better navigate the liminal and create transitional learning spaces is a life skill that is under-discussed and under-practiced. If you're reading this book, you are ahead of the curve. But learning to *stop, ask, explore* is something we can not only utilize ourselves, but also help others to do. I'm not suggesting that you try to teach people while they are in incendiary emotions. That would be like trying to teach someone whose clothes are on fire about stop, drop and roll. Instead, when we get that call from a colleague or friend who is going through it, can we keep from matching their incendiary emotions or giving them advice with no context and encourage them to *stop, ask, explore*? Here are some questions for reflection:

When was a time one of my friends or colleagues asked for advice or called to vent when they were in a What Now? Moment?

Did I give advice? Listen? Console? Other?

If I received a call tomorrow from a person having a What Now? Moment, would it be helpful to do it differently?

How might I use *stop, ask, explore* with my team at work?

Could this be useful with my family?

Living in the liminal

Uncertain times call for new ways of being and doing. The paradox of living in a creative and generative way in uncharted territory is that we need to be at once incredibly humble and, at the same time, bold. We need to be willing to explore, but not get distracted and lost in searching. We need to be ready to have the rug pulled out from under us as the future of work, technology, cultural shifts, climate change, and social and economic challenges require us to adjust and adapt to a world that is constantly changing.

The name of this book was supposed to be *Flux*. I did the due diligence, bought the URL, and spent more than two years kneading the insights and approaches you've read about here into a proposal that captured the imagination of my editors and resulted in a book deal. We created graphics and wrote the blurbs. And, about a week before we were set to approve the cover design, I got a note from someone I encountered randomly online who said, "I noticed in your bio that you have a book coming out named *Flux*—so does my friend." She included a link to a book that was scheduled for release about four months before mine. Completely different content, but the same title.

This was, as you might imagine, a What Now? Moment for me. I was writing on a very aggressive and tight deadline and, taking my own medicine, I needed to stop writing to ask myself (and my editorial team) what the best path forward from there might be. There is something wonderful in the creative process when we get to use our research and theories in practice, which I do every day. To test it in our own spaces to see if what we observe in others comes to roost in our own lives. As I stopped for two weeks (which felt like an eternity if I had any shot at keeping to my writing deadlines) and considered how a title shift at that stage would affect the process, I was also able to see how other people processed my challenge.

I was able to see how my dispassionate curiosity landed with others—and they didn't like it. "You must be so upset," they told me. "Keep the name and fight it out... your book will be better than the other one, hold your ground."

All of that advice was delivered with just the sort of incendiary emotions I was tamping down in myself as I stopped, composed myself, gained my bearings, and reconsidered how I wanted to position the work and how what I knew about the other work (which wasn't much) might influence how I thought about the space between my own What Now? and what comes next. This got me thinking more about flux in general and the flux that is created in our own minds and in the minds of others who make our flux their own.

This What Now? Moment expanded and put a fine point on my aspiration for this work to be more than a "self-help" or "professional development" tool. Sure, it is my hope that people will use it to get much better at navigating their own What Now? Moments. But it also can support us in helping others when they engage us in their inflection points. Like the end result of so many What Now? Moments, the shift from "flux" to *Stop, Ask, Explore,* the new title I ultimately settled on, was a blessing in disguise. Times had changed drastically since those earlier drafts of the book. In 2021, nobody in the world needed to be convinced (or reminded!) that we are living in times of flux. Instead, *Stop, Ask, Explore* is meant to point toward potential solutions. Not in a prescriptive way, but as a clarion call for us to pay attention to our relationship with change and uncertainty and learn to embrace it as a route to growth and learning, even when it is frightening and uncomfortable. It invites us to think about who we are, where we are going, and how those two questions come together to help us in the simple, very human task of willfinding and wayfinding through life together.

Parting words

Whether we like it or not, we are living through uncertain times—and there's more to embracing it than training ourselves to respond to the unexpected. The approaches and practices we discuss in this book are an invitation for each and every one of us to become a trailblazer. An adventurer. An explorer with the willingness to ask new questions and experiment with new ways of being as we travel through life's calms and storms. A wayfinder.

So, even if external flux settles (which is unlikely any time soon), the natural rhythm of a life well lived invites us to learn, discern, choose, and confirm over and over again. If we can learn to choose the curiosity loop over the fear loop and proceed with an experimental mindset, this can become less and less challenging with each point of transition or change. The more we learn to trust our ability to suss things out—whether or not we know exactly where we're going—the more comfortable navigating transitions becomes. *Stop, Ask, Explore* is about embracing wayfinding as a way of life to learn to flourish even when the going gets tough. If we accept that change is inevitable, and we are up to the task of navigating it, we can create our own frameworks for future action that lead to success and personal wellbeing, however we choose to define them.

This book is not about motivation. It is not meant to give you a shot of dopamine and get you pumped up to make a change, only to get caught up in the day-to-day again and shift yourself back into whatever groove you were in before you picked it up. The kind of inquiry that I'm inviting you to (or, for those of you who were already at it, to pause and consider) is something different. In the same way that deciding to climb a mountain or start a business or run for elected office is the beginning of a much longer process, the premise of *Stop, Ask, Explore* is for it to spark possibility—and underscore that preparation, development, resourcing, and an inclination to dispassionate curiosity and learning in practice are the skills and capacities we need to flourish in uncharted territory. And the 2020s are clearly uncharted territory.

So, as we close, I invite you to view this as the beginning, not the end. This is not about coming away from this with five easy steps, seven new ideals or ten superpowers to make all of your dreams come true. It is about a simple recognition that living in uncertain times—whether that be at the grassroots or global level of assessment—calls for a new set of skills and capacities.

And that will take more than simply learning to navigate change in uncertain times. It is the recognition that, as human beings navigating the world around us, we are exploring identities, getting our bearings and trying to flourish as we pursue our self-world fit. And so is everyone else.

So, What Now?

Conclusion

I came across Rob Freer's post on LinkedIn just a few days before I completed the manuscript for this book. I had notes in hand and a structure in place for what I thought would be the conclusion and decided to delete all of it when he agreed to allow me to share his heartfelt post in full here. I'll let Rob tell you who he is and where he is on his journey. He writes:

I resigned.

After nine and a half years at a large wine and spirits company, I have decided enough is enough. I intentionally gave up a successful career and steady paycheck because I need a break.

I resigned because I am burned out from a position that I feel is too much for one person to be successful, with a relentless volume of work.

I resigned because I felt undervalued, getting paid ~20% less than my counterparts.

I resigned because I hated that I would start to get annoyed at my kids for procrastinating in the morning because I had to get to my computer to reply to emails.

I resigned because I need to slow down and take a break, not to wake up at 5 a.m. and have checking emails be the first thing I do.

This has been one of the biggest decisions of my career, leaving stability for the unknown.

This might be the best, or worst, decision for my career, however I am betting on myself, and I am curious about what a different future this will lead to.

I am going to miss the teams I worked with day in and day out, my friends and work family. Many have wished me the best. Many have said they would recommend me. Many have said it takes guts to what I'm doing. Some have said they might not be far behind.

I will miss the human connection, so if there are people out there that want to chat, reach out. I've got nothing but time. Whether it is about what I am doing, or you have a question about the spirits industry feel free to send me a message.

As for what is next? Who knows? I am going to take some time, reflect, recharge and rebuild. I will come out stronger and happier for doing this.

In choosing to stop, ask new questions, and explore new options for his work and life, Rob is embarking on a wayfinder's journey – whether or not he would use that language. And he is not alone. In the wake of a tumultuous start to the 2020s, millions of people around the globe have chosen, or been forced, to pause and reflect on who they are and what matters to them. Some believe that these moves are a knee-jerk reaction to pandemic shutdowns and a global forced pause we've not seen in modern history. While that may be true, this great resignation, or reshuffle, or reorientation in our tech-fueled world has been happening for more than a decade. It fueled the stuckness that catalyzed the research that laid the groundwork for this book, and it will continue to require us to stop, ask new questions and explore new routes forward as we adapt to a changing landscape across the 2020s and beyond.

So how do we live in these tumultuous times? What resources do we need, individually and collectively, to create (and recreate) the systems we need to flourish rather than simply survive the world we are creating? How do we orient ourselves in this uncharted territory?

I've learned a lot about navigating change in uncertain times over the past decade, and there are many more questions that I will continue to pursue in the coming years. In fact, it is my deep hope that anyone reading this book who is interested in participating in this inquiry with me will engage with me in future research—as an individual or with your team. Whether you choose to join me on this quest, or you are more interested in continuing your inquiry in your own context, the most important thing is to view the end of this book as the beginning of a new relationship with change in uncertain times.

This is the exciting, and perhaps arduous, task facing every one of us in this early part of the of the 21st century. The new explorers who know and accept (maybe kicking and screaming) that the future lives in yet-to-be-imagined systems and processes for which there are no best practices and past successes to rely upon—or even rebel against. Reading these pages and engaging with the corresponding materials may have inspired you to slow down or speed up. You may be experimenting with some new things, or you may have made some concrete decisions. The work may inspire you to make a big change or to confirm that the path you're on is the one for you. There is no possible way that I could know the capacities you need to build, the resources you need to gather, or the changes you need to consider to get from where you are to where you hope to go. I have no idea what goals your organization and team are pursuing, or how you define success and what sacrifices you are willing to make to achieve it. You might not know that either. And it's into that unknown that we venture together.

These are the questions that drive my work in the world with people like Rob—and perhaps like you—who are choosing to see things differently and are willing to carve out new ways of working and being in the years to come. My dream is for the wayfinders of the world to find one another. To support one another. To share resources and ideas. What's worked and what hasn't. We can share what we are learning with one another. That is why this book is not about answers. Answers are too certain. Too absolute. Instead, let's raise questions together and create learning spaces that will uncover what it takes for companies to become places where people can do meaningful and productive work *and* flourish outside of it. Let's share insights and resources that will help light the way for those among us who are lost in the thick of the woods.

I invite you to join a growing community of wayfinders who are, by choice or circumstance, learning to navigate change in uncertain times by both exploring new ways to do things *and* using tried and true tools together to move from times of execution to exploration and back again. Whether you are a student transitioning from college to career, an early-career professional with an ambition to do work you love, or an established leader creating the future of work right now, recognizing the liminal space as a transitional—and potentially transformational—learning space is at the core of what I'm hoping to accomplish by sharing my work at this stage of my inquiry. If you choose to continue on this journey, I hope you've come away with some new perspectives to help guide you on your way. Some will resonate. Others will not. That is to be expected—and it is welcomed—since the wayfinding task we all face in this moment in history is to chart our own course and gather the relevant resources we need to follow it.

So please don't engage this work to add another checklist of activities to your already busy schedule. Instead, let's learn together what it takes enter the unknown with a sense of adventure. Let's find new ways to help one other to shape organizations, communities and lives built for the pursuit of human flourishing. Let's commit to becoming willing and finding new ways to enter the unknown without a true north, compass or maps upon which to rely. And let's do it with an acknowledgement that despite the politics and the environment and the discord and the loans and the ageism and the economy, we are not doomed. Nor can we rely on the magic of positive thinking. Sure, the terrain might not feel very accommodating and change may be uncomfortable, but this is the straw we've pulled as human beings born in this time in this place. So, like so many others born before us to uncertain times, we need to examine ourselves and determine how we want to live, what meaning we hope to bring to bear on the circumstances we're facing and what it will mean to flourish in this new environment—in practice not just theory. That means asking ourselves new kinds of questions and creating spaces to answer them.

Questions like:

- If turning points inspire a threat response, how might we equip ourselves and our teams to face them?
- If perceptions of threat create unhelpful emotional and behavioral responses in ourselves and our teams, how might we reframe it?
- If fear leads to impulsive reactions and hopelessness in the face of uncertain transitions and change, how do we turn it around and engage uncertainty with an exploratory mindset (even when we feel under-resourced or find ourselves operating in unhelpful systems)?

I don't offer these questions as a matter of navel gazing or self-enlightenment. These are concrete and practical questions meant to prompt preparation for unrelenting change. A practice of active resilience that will equip future leaders working at every scale for the tasks they are called to—in service of others and on their own wayfinding journeys. And we all need to be equipped. Whether you take on key issues and wicked problems at a global level, a regional level, or in your neighborhood or home, we need to recognize that, in addition to critical challenges like climate change, poverty, social unrest and inequality of every kind, there are new What Now? Moments on the horizon that are, as yet, beyond our imagining—and we need wayfinders with the resources, hope and experimental mindset to understand how to approach the opportunities and challenges we'll face in the 2020s and beyond with creativity, humility and care.

And the 2020s are going to be a wild ride.

Built on a foundation shaken by a global pandemic, political and social unrest, and mass adoption of technology for work and life, we stand together at a massive point of inflection. Ours is not the first What Now? Moment. Countless humans have stood at points of inflection throughout history asking the same questions that our ancestors across the globe have asked for millennia. Who are we? What does it mean to live a good life? Where do we go from here? These questions become even more poignant in the context of emerging massive changes we'll be dealing with over the coming decades.

Technology, science and virtual reality

We're on the brink of a massive shift in what we perceive to be real. I'm not just talking about gaming headsets. Artificial intelligence, machine learning, the blockchain, quantum computing, VR and AR, the Internet of Things, robotics—these technologies that are much discussed in blogging and podcast circles are already changing the fabric of fields as varied as healthcare, law, education, manufacturing, art and others. As we move closer to the convergence of these technologies on every aspect of our lives, the human toll remains unknown. How will we think about equity, access, and the distribution of resources and power that will come into question as these technologies become adopted more widely? What will it mean for how we work and how we live together if we are inter-acting and engaging in multiple realities with our interactions mediated by machines? How will we address the gaps between those with access to these technologies and those without access?

Lifelong learning in an untrustworthy reality

The life cycle of skills and capacities to operate in these new reali-ties is shorter and shorter every year. This means that more people need to keep up with more information more frequently than ever before in human history. While we like to believe that having access to information means that we will be more educated, the way that information flows and is driven by algorithms means that we are increasingly receiving our information in echo cham-bers that can make even the most educated and interested people question whether the information they are receiving is accurate, trustworthy and complete. This means that it will become increas-ingly difficult for people to get and keep their bearings, even if we create global education systems. What does it mean to go to university if we no longer trust educators? How do we learn online if we don't trust platforms? How do we adapt to an evolv-ing understanding of history, power, diversity and inclusion and apply that understanding to bring about equality and justice in our systems, organizations and communities?

Healthcare, mental health and humanity

According to data collected by the UN, the average lifespan of human beings globally has increased by 20 years since the 1960s, and the trend is on the rise (Ruggeri, 2018). More people living longer, and healthier lives is a wonderful outcome of modern science. But what do our societies look like when living to 100+ is normal? How do our systems and societies deal with life spans that extend 30 or 40 years beyond traditional retirement? How do we make space for one another and develop the systems we need to accommodate an older population, not only for physical health but for mental health? What are the implications for the planet, the economy, education systems? How will the technologies mentioned previously influence the way we live and die—especially if we become able to extend our minds into virtual spaces after our bodies are no longer able to sustain us? What does this mean for how we think about what it means to be human?

These things may seem like science fiction, but many are already in existence today—and they are just the tip of the iceberg. The further these technologies go, the further we (and the AIs) will take them. Keeping up with the pace of change is about more than creating new and better training programs at the local employment center. We stand on the brink of unimaginable uncharted territory—and the need for a global community of wayfinders to help make sense of it has never been greater.

I leave you with one final image (Figure 12.1) to guide your wayfinding journey and remind you that the curiosity loop and space for liminal learning is available to you. I hope I can count you among the fold.

FIGURE 12.1 Wayfinder's framework

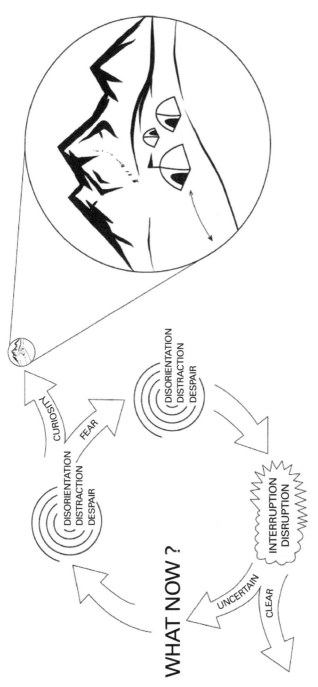

Appendices

Appendix A
Emotion regulation

Emotion regulation is a rich and diverse field of research that continues to evolve as we learn more about the psychological, physiological, philosophical, and cultural aspects of emotions and how they affect our thoughts, behaviour and self-concept. The following books and articles provide a stepping-off point for deeper exploration. This is not intended to be a complete list of relevant sources on this topic. It is, however, a representative sample of the resources that have helped to shape my thinking in the current research.

Books

How Emotions are Made: The secret life of the brain, Lisa Feldman Barrett

The Upside of Stress: Why stress is good for you, and how to get good at it, Kelly McGonigal, PhD

Emotional Agility: Get unstuck, embrace change, and thrive in work and life, Susan David, PhD

The Unapologetic Guide to Black Mental Health: Navigate an unequal system, learn tools for emotional wellness, and get the help you deserve, Rheeda Walker, PhD

The Gift of Fear: Survival signals that protect us from violence, Gavin de Becker

The Managed Heart: Commercialization of human feeling, Arlie Russell Hochschild

Handbook of Positive Emotions, Michele M Tugade, Michelle N Shiota and Leslie D Kirby

Handbook of Emotion Regulation, edited James J Gross

Unstuck: Your guide to the seven-stage journey out of depression, James S Gordon, MD

Relevant academic articles

Aldao, A (2013) The future of emotion regulation research: Capturing context, *Perspectives on Psychological Science*, 8 (2) pp 155–72

Dewick, P, Hofstetter, JS and Schröder, P (2021) From panic to dispassionate rationality—Organizational responses in procurement after the initial COVID-19 pandemic peak, *IEEE Engineering Management Review*, 49 (2) pp 45–56

Feinberg, M, Ford, BQ and Flynn, FJ (2020) Rethinking reappraisal: The double-edged sword of regulating negative emotions in the workplace, *Organizational Behavior and Human Decision Processes*, 161, pp 1–19

Ford, BQ and Troy, AS (2019) Reappraisal reconsidered: A closer look at the costs of an acclaimed emotion-regulation strategy, *Current Directions in Psychological Science*, 28 (2) pp 195–203

Ford, BQ Gross, JJ and Gruber, J (2019) Broadening our field of view: The role of emotion polyregulation, *Emotion Review*, 11 (3) pp 197–208

Ganesh, S (2014) Unraveling the confessional tale: Passion and dispassion in fieldwork, *Management Communication Quarterly*, 28 (3) pp 448–57

Gross, JJ (2001) Emotion regulation in adulthood: Timing is everything, *Current Directions in Psychological Science*, 10 (6) pp 214–19

Gross, JJ and Feldman Barrett, L (2011) Emotion generation and emotion regulation: One or two depends on your point of view, *Emotion review*, 3 (1) pp 8–16

Linton, JC, Kommor, MJ and Webb, CH (1993) Helping the helpers: The development of a critical incident stress management team through university/community cooperation, *Annals of Emergency Medicine*, **22** (4) pp 663–68

Maroney, TA and Gross, JJ (2014) The ideal of the dispassionate judge: An emotion regulation perspective, *Emotion Review*, **6** (2) pp 142–51

Ren, S (2021) *Dispassion and the Good Life: A study of Stoicism and Zhuangism* (Doctoral dissertation, Duke University)

Sheppes, G, Scheibe, S, Suri, G, Radu, P, Blechert, J and Gross, JJ (2014) Emotion regulation choice: A conceptual framework and supporting evidence, *Journal of Experimental Psychology: General*, **143** (1) p. 163

Smith, AM, Willroth, EC, Gatchpazian, A, Shallcross, AJ, Feinberg, M and Ford, BQ (2021) Coping with health threats: The costs and benefits of managing emotions, *Psychological Science*, **32** (7) pp 1011–23

Vasilyev, P (2017) Beyond dispassion: Emotions and judicial decision-making in modern Europe, *Rechtsgeschichte-Legal History*, (25) pp 277–85

Webb, TL, Miles, E and Sheeran, P (2012) Dealing with feeling: A meta-analysis of the effectiveness of strategies derived from the process model of emotion regulation, *Psychological Bulletin*, **138** (4) p 775

Appendix B
Resilience

Resilience is a rich and diverse field of research that crosses disciplines and levels of analysis, from the individual to the community and ecosystem. The following books and articles provide a stepping-off point for deeper exploration. This is not intended to be a complete list of relevant sources on this topic. It is, however, a representative sample of the resources that have helped to shape my thinking in the current research.

Books

Change Your World: The science of resilience and the true path to success, Michael Ungar, PhD

Being Wrong: Adventures in the margin of error, Kathryn Schulz

Better by Mistake: The unexpected benefits of being wrong, Alina Tugend

Flourish: A visionary new understanding of happiness and well-being, Martin Seligman

Executive Resilience: Neuroscience for the business of disruption, Jurie G Rossouw with Pieter J Rossouw

Antifragile: Things that gain from disorder, Massim Nicholas Taleb

Psychological Capital and Beyond, Fred Luthans, Carolyn M. Youssef-Morgan and Bruce Avolio

Character Strengths and Virtues: A handbook and classification, Christopher Peterson and Martin EP Seligman

Relevant academic articles

Ayala, JC and Manzano, G (2014) The resilience of the entrepreneur: Influence on the success of the business, A longitudinal analysis, *Journal of Economic Psychology*, **42**, pp 126–35

Ball, J and Lamberton, C (2015) Rising every time they fall: The importance and determinants of consumer resilience, *ACR North American Advances*, pp 191–96

Bartone, PT (2006) Resilience under military operational stress: Can leaders influence hardiness?, *Military Psychology*, **18** (S) pp S131–48

Beutel, ME, Glaesmer, H, Decker, O, Fischbeck, S and Brähler, E (2009) Life satisfaction, distress, and resiliency across the life span of women, *Menopause*, **16** (6), pp 1132–38

Bonanno, GA (2004) Loss, trauma, and human resilience: Have we underestimated the human capacity to thrive after extremely aversive events?, *American Psychologist*, **59** (1), pp 20–28

Brougham, RR, Zail, CM, Mendoza, CM and Miller, JR (2009) Stress, sex differences, and coping strategies among college students, *Current Psychology*, **28** (2), pp 85–97

Fletcher, D and Sarkar, M (2013) Psychological resilience: a review and critique of definitions, concepts and theory, *European Psychologist*, **18** (1), pp 12–23

Luthar, SS, Cicchetti, D and Becker, B (2000) The construct of resilience: a critical evaluation and guidelines for future work, *Child Development*, **71** (3), pp 543–62

Masten, AS (2001) Ordinary magic: resilience processes in development, *American Psychologist*, **56** (3), pp 227–38

Masten, AS (2007) Resilience in developing systems: progress and promise as the fourth wave rises, *Development and Psychopathology*, **19** (3), pp 921–30

Morales, EE (2008) Exceptional female students of color: academic resilience and gender in higher education, *Innovative Higher Education*, **33** (3), pp 197–213

Morrison, GM and Allen, MR (2007) Promoting student resilience in school contexts, *Theory into Practice,* **46** (2), pp 162–69

Ong, AD, Bergeman, CS, Bisconti, TL and Wallace, KA (2006) Psychological resilience, positive emotions, and successful adaptation to stress in later life, *Journal of Personality and Social Psychology,* **91** (4), pp 730–49

Richardson, GE (2002) The metatheory of resilience and resiliency, *Journal of Clinical Psychology,* **58** (3), pp 307–321

Rutten, BPF et al (2013) Resilience in mental health: linking psychological and neurobiological perspectives, *Acta Psychiatrica Scandinavica,* **128** (1), pp 3–20

Tugade, MM and Fredrickson, BL (2004) Resilient individuals use positive emotions to bounce back from negative emotional experiences, *Journal of Personality and Social Psychology,* **86** (2), pp 320–33

Tugade, MM, Fredrickson, BL and Barrett, LF (2004) Psychological resilience and positive emotional granularity: examining the benefits of positive emotions on coping and health, *Journal of Personality,* **72** (6), pp 1161–90

Windle, G (2011) What is resilience? A review and concept analysis, *Reviews in Clinical Gerontology,* **21** (2), pp 152–69

Appendix C
Conceptual metaphor

The study of conceptual metaphor and the influence it has on the way we think, behave and frame our understanding of ourselves and the world around us is a well-established, but still evolving field of study. The following books and articles provide a stepping-off point for deeper exploration. This is not intended to be a complete list of relevant sources on this topic. It is, however, a representative sample of the resources that have helped to shape my thinking in the current research.

Books

Metaphors We Live By, George Lakoff and Mark Johnson
Marketing Metaphoria: What deep metaphors reveal about the minds of consumers, Gerald and Lindsay Zaltman
I Never Metaphor I Didn't Like: A comprehensive compilation of history's greatest analogies, metaphors and similes, Dr. Mardy Grothe
I is an Other, The Secret Life of Metaphor and How it Shapes the Way We See the World, James Geary

Relevant academic articles

Amin, TG (2009) Conceptual metaphor meets conceptual change, *Human Development*, 52 (3) pp 165–97
Amin, TG (2015) Conceptual metaphor and the study of conceptual change: Research synthesis and future directions, *International Journal of Science Education*, 37 (5–6) pp 966–91

Ball, J (2019) Ecosystems, Blueprints and Journeys–Oh My! Toward a practice-oriented typology of service design metaphors, *Touchpoint*, **11**, pp 70–76

Caballero, R and Ibarretxe-Antuñano, I (2009) Ways of perceiving, moving, and thinking: Revindicating culture in conceptual metaphor research, *Cognitive Semiotics*, **5** (1–2) pp 268–90

Casasanto, D (2009) When is a linguistic metaphor a conceptual metaphor? *New Directions in Cognitive Linguistics*, **24**, pp 127–45

Christensen, GL and Olson, JC (2002) Mapping consumers' mental models with ZMET, *Psychology & Marketing*, **19** (6) pp 477–501

Close, HG and Scherr, RE (2015) Enacting conceptual metaphor through blending: Learning activities embodying the substance metaphor for energy, *International Journal of Science Education*, **37** (5–6) pp 839–66

Danesi, M (2007) A conceptual metaphor framework for the teaching of mathematics, *Studies in Philosophy and Education*, **26** (3) pp 225–36

Daane, AR, Haglund, J, Robertson, AD, Close, HG and Scherr, RE (2018) The pedagogical value of conceptual metaphor for secondary science teachers, *Science Education*, **102** (5) pp 1051–76

Flensner, KK and Von der Lippe, M (2019) Being safe from what and safe for whom? A critical discussion of the conceptual metaphor of 'safe space', *Intercultural Education*, **30** (3) pp 275–288

Gibbs Jr, RW (2011) Evaluating conceptual metaphor theory, *Discourse Processes*, **48** (8) pp 529–62

Howie, P and Bagnall, R (2013) A beautiful metaphor: Transformative learning theory, *International Journal of Lifelong Education*, **32** (6) pp 816–36

Ibarretxe-Antuñano, I (2013) The relationship between conceptual metaphor and culture, *Intercultural Pragmatics*, **10** (2) pp 315–39

Kövecses, Z (2008) Conceptual metaphor theory: Some criticisms and alternative proposals, *Annual Review of Cognitive Linguistics*, **6** (1) pp 168–84

Kövecses, Z (2016) Conceptual metaphor theory. In *The Routledge Handbook of Metaphor and Language* (pp 31–45) Routledge

Kövecses, Z (2020) *Extended Conceptual Metaphor Theory*, Cambridge University Press

Lakoff, G and Johnson, M (1980) Conceptual metaphor in everyday language, *The Journal of Philosophy*, 77 (8) pp 453–86

Lakoff, G (1994) What is a conceptual system? *The Nature and Ontogenesis of Meaning*, pp 41–90

Lakoff, G (2008) Conceptual metaphor. In *Cognitive Linguistics: Basic readings* (pp 185–238) De Gruyter Mouton

Lakoff, G and Johnson, M (2020) Conceptual metaphor in everyday language. In *Shaping Entrepreneurship Research* (pp 475–504) Routledge

McGlone, MS (2007) What is the explanatory value of a conceptual metaphor? *Language & Communication*, **27** (2) pp 109–26

Shearer, RL, Aldemir, T, Hitchcock, J, Resig, J, Driver, J and Kohler, M (2020) What students want: A vision of a future online learning experience grounded in distance education theory, *American Journal of Distance Education*, **34** (1) pp 36–52

Slingerland, E (2004) Conceptions of the self in the Zhuangzi: Conceptual metaphor analysis and comparative thought, *Philosophy East and West*, pp 322–42

Soriano, C (2015) Emotion and conceptual metaphor. In *Methods of Exploring Emotions* (pp 226–34) Routledge

Stickles, E, David, O, Dodge, EK and Hong, J (2016) Formalizing contemporary conceptual metaphor theory: A structured repository for metaphor analysis, *Constructions and Frames*, 8 (2) pp 166–213

Vervaeke, J and Kennedy, JM (2004) Conceptual metaphor and abstract thought, *Metaphor and Symbol*, **19** (3) pp 213–31

Wickman, SA, Daniels, MH, White, LJ and Fesmire, SA (1999) A "primer" in conceptual metaphor for counsellors, *Journal of Counseling & Development*, **77** (4) pp 389–94

Appendix D
Transformative learning and threshold concepts

The study of transformative learning and threshold concepts plumbs the depths of how we learn and what it takes to move into and through the learning process, even when it becomes troublesome. The following books and articles provide a stepping-off point for deeper exploration of this topic. This is not intended to be a complete list of relevant sources. It is, however, a representative sample of the resources that have helped to shape my thinking in the current research.

Books

Learning Spaces: Creating opportunities for knowledge creation in academic life, Maggi Savin-Baden

Transformations: Identity construction in contemporary culture, Grant McCracken

Threshold Concepts Within the Disciplines, Ray Land, Jan HF Meyer and Jan Smith (Eds)

The Handbook of Transformative Learning: Theory, research, and practice, Edward W Taylor and Patricia Cranton

The Fifth Discipline: The art and practice of the learning organization, Peter M Senge

A More Beautiful Question: The power of inquiry to spark breakthrough ideas, Warren Berger

Long-Life Learning: Preparing for jobs that don't even exist yet, Michelle R Weise

Curiosity The desire to know and why your future depends on it, Ian Leslie

The Creativity Leap: Unleash curiosity, improvisation, and intuition at work, Natalie Nixon

Insight: Why we're not as self-aware as we think and how seeing ourselves clearly helps us succeed in work and in life, Tasha Eurich

The Rites of Passage (2e), Arnold van Gennep

Relevant academic articles

Aboytes, JGR and Barth, M (2020) Transformative learning in the field of sustainability: A systematic literature review (1999–2019), *International Journal of Sustainability in Higher Education*, pp 993–1013

Alhadeff-Jones, M (2012) Transformative learning and the challenges of complexity, *The Handbook of Transformative Learning: Theory, research, and practice*, pp 178–94

Bishop, K and Etmanski, C (2021) Down the rabbit hole: Creating a transformative learning environment, *Studies in the Education of Adults*, pp 1–13

Bourn, D and Issler, S (2010) Transformative learning for a global society, *Education and Social Change: Connecting local and global perspectives*, pp 225–37

Buechner, B, Dirkx, J, Konvisser, ZD, Myers, D and Peleg-Baker, T (2020) From liminality to communitas: The collective dimensions of transformative learning, *Journal of Transformative Education*, **18** (2) pp 87–113

Christie, M, Carey, M, Robertson, A and Grainger, P (2015) Putting transformative learning theory into practice, *Australian Journal of Adult Learning*, **55** (1) pp 9–30

Elias, D (1997) It's time to change our minds: An introduction to transformative learning, *ReVision*, **20** (1) pp 2–7

Fleming, T (2018) Mezirow and the theory of transformative learning. In *Critical Theory and Transformative Learning* (pp 120–36) IGI Global

Gouthro, P (2018) Creativity, the arts, and transformative learning. In *The Palgrave International Handbook on Adult and Lifelong Education and Learning* (pp 1011–26) Palgrave Macmillan, London

Groen, J and Kawalilak, C (2016) Creating spaces for transformative learning in the workplace, *New Directions for Adult and Continuing Education*, 2016 (152) pp 61–71

Howie, P and Bagnall, R (2013) A beautiful metaphor: Transformative learning theory, *International Journal of Lifelong Education*, 32 (6) pp 816–36

Land, R, Rattray, J and Vivian, P (2014) Learning in the liminal space: A semiotic approach to threshold concepts, *Higher Education*, 67 (2) pp 199–217

Lange, E (2015) Transformative learning and concepts of the self: Insights from immigrant and intercultural journeys, *International Journal of Lifelong Education*, 34 (6) pp 623–42

Lee, N, Irving, C and Francuz, J (2014) Community-embedded learning and experimentation: Fostering spaces for transformative learning online. In A Nicolaides and D Holt (Eds), *Spaces of transformation and transformation of Space: Proceedings of XI International Transformative Learning Conference*, Teachers College, Columbia University, New York, October 24–26, 2014, (pp 499–506)

Mälkki, K and Green, L (2014) Navigational aids: The phenomenology of transformative learning, *Journal of Transformative Education*, 12 (1) pp 5–24

Martin, SD, Snow, JL and Franklin Torrez, CA (2011) Navigating the terrain of third space: Tensions with/in relationships in school-university partnerships, *Journal of Teacher Education*, 62 (3) pp 299–311

Morgan, AD (2010) Journeys into transformation: Travel to an "other" place as a vehicle for transformative learning, *Journal of Transformative Education*, **8** (4) pp 246–68

Nye, A and Clark, J (2016) "Being and becoming" a researcher: Building a reflective environment to create a transformative learning experience for undergraduate students, *Journal of Transformative Education*, **14** (4) pp 377–91

Savin-Baden, M, McFarland, L and Savin-Baden, J (2008) Learning spaces, agency and notions of improvement: What influences thinking and practices about teaching and learning in higher education? An interpretive meta-ethnography, *London Review of Education*, **6** (3) pp 211–27

Savin-Baden, M (2008) Liquid learning and troublesome spaces: Journeys from the threshold? In *Threshold Concepts Within the Disciplines* (pp 75–88) Brill Sense

Schnitzler, T (2019) The bridge between education for sustainable development and transformative learning: Towards new collaborative learning spaces, *Journal of Education for Sustainable Development*, **13** (2) pp 242–53

Selby, D, Selby, D and Kagawa, F (2015) Thoughts from a darkened corner: Transformative learning for the gathering storm, *Sustainability Frontiers: Critical and transformative voices from the borderlands of sustainability education*, pp 21–42

Simm, D and Marvell, A (2015) Gaining a "sense of place": Students' affective experiences of place leading to transformative learning on international fieldwork, *Journal of Geography in Higher Education*, **39** (4) pp 595–616

Taylor, PC (2013) Research as transformative learning for meaning-centred professional development, *Meaning-Centred Education: International perspectives and explorations in higher education*, pp 168–85

Ukpokodu, O (2009) The practice of transformative pedagogy, *Journal on Excellence in College Teaching*, **20** (2) pp 43–67 van Dellen, T and Cohen-Scali, V (2015) The transformative potential of workplace learning: Construction of identity in learning spaces, *International Review of Education*, **61**, pp 725–34

Watkins Jr, CE, Davis, EC and Callahan, JL (2018) On disruption, disorientation, and development in clinical supervision: A transformative learning perspective, *The Clinical Supervisor*, **37** (2) pp 257–77

Appendix E
Sensemaking

Sensemaking is a rich and varied field of study and practice that has several distinct streams of research and practice. The following books, articles and communities of learning and practice provide a stepping-off point for deeper exploration of sensemaking. This is not intended to be a complete list of relevant sources. It is, however, a representative sample of the resources that helped to shape my thinking in the current research.

Books

Cynefin: Weaving sense-making into the fabric of our world, Dave Snowden and friends

Rethinking Design Thinking: Making sense of the future that has already arrived, GK VanPatter

Managing the Unexpected (3e): Sustained performance in a complex world, Karl E Weick and Kathleen M Sutcliffe

Sensemaking in Organizations, Karl E Weick

Making Sense of the Organization, Karl E Weick

Transitions: Making sense of life's changes, William Bridges, PhD with Susan Bridges

Applied Imagination: Principles and procedures of creative problem solving, Alex Osborn

Range: Why generalists triumph in a specialized world, David Epstein

Small Data: The tiny clues that uncover huge trends, Martin Lindstrom

Relevant academic articles

Barry, D and Meisiek, S (2010) Seeing more and seeing differently: Sensemaking, mindfulness, and the workarts, *Organization Studies*, **31** (11) pp 1505–30

Böhler, D (2014) Order creation from a transactional perspective: Creating practices from sensemaking processes. In *On the Nature of Distributed Organizing* (pp 57–67) Springer Gabler, Wiesbaden

Brown, AD, Stacey, P and Nandhakumar, J (2008) Making sense of sensemaking narratives, *Human Relations*, **61** (8) pp 1035–62

Brown, AD (2000) Making sense of inquiry sensemaking, *Journal of Management Studies*, **37** (1) pp 45–75

Christianson, MK and Barton, MA (2020) Sensemaking in the time of COVID-19, *Journal of Management Studies*, **58** (2), pp 572–76

Colville, ID, Waterman, RH and Weick, KE (1999) Organizing and the search for excellence: Making sense of the times in theory and practice, *Organization*, **6** (1) pp 129–48

Craig-Lees, M (2001) Sense making: Trojan horse? Pandora's box? *Psychology & Marketing*, **18** (5) pp 513–26

Drazin, R, Glynn, MA and Kazanjian, RK (1999) Multilevel theorizing about creativity in organizations: A sensemaking perspective, *Academy of Management Review*, **24** (2) pp 286–307

Gioia, DA and Thomas, JB (1996) Identity, image, and issue interpretation: Sensemaking during strategic change in academia, *Administrative Science Quarterly*, pp 370–403

Gioia, DA and Chittipeddi, K (1991) Sensemaking and sensegiving in strategic change initiation, *Strategic Management Journal*, **12** (6) pp 433–48

Holt, R and Cornelissen, J (2014) Sensemaking revisited, *Management Learning*, **45** (5) pp 525–39

Kezar, A and Eckel, P (2002) Examining the institutional transformation process: The importance of sensemaking, interrelated strategies, and balance, *Research in Higher Education*, **43** (3) pp 295–328

Kurtz, CF and Snowden, DJ (2003) The new dynamics of strategy: Sense-making in a complex and complicated world, *IBM Systems Journal*, **42** (3) pp 462–83

Lüscher, LS and Lewis, MW (2008) Organizational change and managerial sensemaking: Working through paradox, *Academy of Management Journal*, **51** (2) pp 221–40

Lynam, T and Fletcher, C (2015) Sensemaking: A complexity perspective. *Ecology and Society*, **20** (1)

Maitlis, S, Vogus, TJ and Lawrence, TB (2013) Sensemaking and emotion in organizations, *Organizational Psychology Review*, **3** (3) pp 222–47

Mills, JH, Thurlow, A and Mills, AJ (2010) Making sense of sensemaking: The critical sensemaking approach, *Qualitative Research in Organizations and Management: An International Journal*, **5** (2) pp 182–95

Moore, DT and Hoffman, RR (2011) Sensemaking: A transformative paradigm, *American Intelligence Journal*, **29** (1) pp 26–36

Osland, JS and Bird, A (2000) Beyond sophisticated stereotyping: Cultural sensemaking in context, *Academy of Management Perspectives*, **14** (1) pp 65–77

Patriotta, G (2003) Sensemaking on the shop floor: Narratives of knowledge in organizations, *Journal of Management Studies*, **40** (2) pp 349–75

Pye, A (2005) Leadership and organizing: Sensemaking in action, *Leadership*, **1** (1) pp 31–49

Schildt, H, Mantere, S and Cornelissen, J (2020) Power in sensemaking processes, *Organization Studies*, **41** (2) pp 241–65

Schwandt, DR (2005) When managers become philosophers: Integrating learning with sensemaking, *Academy of Management Learning & Education*, **4** (2) pp 176–92

Seligman, L (2006) Sensemaking throughout adoption and the innovation-decision process, *European Journal of Innovation Management*, **9** (1), pp 108–20

Sharma, N (2006) Sensemaking: Bringing theories and tools together, *Proceedings of the American Society for Information Science and Technology*, **43** (1) pp 1–8

Snowden, D (2002) Complex acts of knowing: paradox and descriptive self-awareness, *Journal of Knowledge Management*, **6** (2) pp 100–111

Snowden, D (2005) Multi-ontology sense making: A new simplicity in decision making, *Journal of Innovation in Health Informatics*, **13** (1) pp 45–53

Snowden, D (2011) Naturalizing sensemaking. In *Informed by Knowledge* (pp 237–48) Psychology Press

Steigenberger, N (2015) Emotions in sensemaking: A change management perspective, *Journal of Organizational Change Management*, **28** (3) pp 432–51

Thomas, JB, Clark, SM and Gioia, DA (1993) Strategic sensemaking and organizational performance: Linkages among scanning, interpretation, action, and outcomes, *Academy of Management Journal*, **36** (2) pp 239–70

Thurlow, A and Mills, JH (2009) Change, talk and sensemaking, *Journal of Organizational Change Management*, **22** (5) pp 459–79

Weick, KE (2005) Managing the unexpected: Complexity as distributed sensemaking. In *Uncertainty and Surprise in Complex Systems* (pp 51–65) Springer, Berlin, Heidelberg

Weick, K, Sutcliffe, K and Obstfeld, D (2009) Organizing and the process of sensemaking, *Handbook of Decision Making*, **16** (4) p 83

Weick, KE (2012) Organized sensemaking: A commentary on processes of interpretive work, *Human Relations*, **65** (1) pp 141–53

Whiteman, G and Cooper, WH (2011) Ecological sensemaking, *Academy of Management Journal*, **54** (5) pp 889–911

Wright, CR, Manning, MR, Farmer, B and Gilbreath, B (2000) Resourceful sensemaking in product development teams, *Organization Studies*, **21** (4) pp 807–25

Wrzesniewski, A, Dutton, JE and Debebe, G (2003) Interpersonal sensemaking and the meaning of work, *Research in Organizational Behavior*, **25**, pp 93–135

Communities of learning and practice

Cognitive Edge: https://thecynefin.co/

The International Bateson Institute: https://batesoninstitute.org/

Humantific: https://www.humantific.com/

The Grey Swan Guild: https://www.greyswanguild.org/

Appendix F
Wayfinding and navigation

Wayfinding and navigation research crosses between two primary domains: the design of interior and exterior spaces, and spatial orientation in real and virtual environments. The following books and articles provide a stepping-off point for deeper exploration of wayfinding and navigation in both of those streams. This is not intended to be a complete list of relevant sources. It is, however, a representative sample of the resources that have helped to shape my thinking in the current research.

Books

Wayfinding: The science and mystery of how humans navigate the world, MR O'Connor
Discernment, Henri Nouwen
From Here to There: The art and science of finding and losing our way, Michael Bond
The Lost Art of Finding Our Way, John Edward Huth
Lead from the Outside: How to build your future and make real change, Stacey Abrams
Finding Your Way Without a Map or Compass, Harold Gatty
Pinpoint: How GPS is changing technology, culture, and our minds, Greg Milner
Design for the Real World: Human ecology and social change, Victor Papanek
Wayfinding: People, signs and architecture, Paul Arthur and Romedi Passini
Biomimicry: Innovation inspired by nature, Janine M Benyus
Entangled Life: How fungi make our worlds, change our minds and shape our futures, Merlin Sheldrake

Relevant academic articles

Allen, GL (1999) Cognitive abilities in the service of wayfinding: A functional approach, *The Professional Geographer*, 51 (4) pp 555–61

Ball, J and Barnes, DC (2017) Delight and the grateful customer: Beyond joy and surprise, *Journal of Service Theory and Practice*, 27 (1), pp 250–69

Blades, M (1991) Wayfinding theory and research: The need for a new approach. In *Cognitive and Linguistic Aspects of Geographic Space* (pp 137–65) Springer, Dordrecht

Cornell, EH, Heth, CD and Rowat, WL (1992) Wayfinding by children and adults: Response to instructions to use lookback and retrace strategies, *Developmental Psychology*, 28 (2) pp 328–36

Cornell, EH, Sorenson, A and Mio, T (2003) Human sense of direction and wayfinding, *Annals of the Association of American Geographers*, 93 (2) pp 399–425

Dalton, RC, Hölscher, C and Montello, DR (2019) Wayfinding as a social activity, *Frontiers in Psychology*, 10, p 142

Darken, RP and Peterson, B (2002) Spatial orientation, wayfinding, and representation. In *Handbook of Virtual Environments* (pp 533–58) CRC Press

Devlin, AS and Bernstein, J (1995) Interactive wayfinding: Use of cues by men and women, *Journal of Environmental Psychology*, 15 (1) pp 23–38

Farr, AC, Kleinschmidt, T, Yarlagadda, P and Mengersen, K (2012) Wayfinding: A simple concept, a complex process, *Transport Reviews*, 32 (6) pp 715–43

Giannopoulos, I, Kiefer, P, Raubal, M, Richter, KF and Thrash, T (2014) Wayfinding decision situations: A conceptual model and evaluation. In *International Conference on Geographic Information Science* (pp 221–34) Springer, Cham

Golledge, RG (1992) Place recognition and wayfinding: Making sense of space, *Geoforum*, **23** (2) pp 199–214

Golledge, RG, Klatzky, RL and Loomis, JM (1996) Cognitive mapping and wayfinding by adults without vision. In *The Construction of Cognitive Maps* (pp 215–46) Springer, Dordrecht

Hartley, T, Maguire, EA, Spiers, HJ and Burgess, N (2003) The well-worn route and the path less traveled: Distinct neural bases of route following and wayfinding in humans, *Neuron*, **37** (5) pp 877–88

Head, D and Isom, M (2010) Age effects on wayfinding and route learning skills, *Behavioural Brain Research*, **209** (1) pp 49–58

Hund, AM and Minarik, JL (2006) Getting from here to there: Spatial anxiety, wayfinding strategies, direction type, and wayfinding efficiency, *Spatial Cognition and Computation*, **6** (3) pp 179–201

Jamshidi, S and Pati, D (2021) A narrative review of theories of wayfinding within the interior environment, *HERD: Health Environments Research & Design Journal*, **14** (1) pp 290–303

Kato, Y and Takeuchi, Y (2003) Individual differences in wayfinding strategies, *Journal of Environmental Psychology*, **23** (2) pp 171–88

Klippel, A (2003) Wayfinding choremes. In *International Conference on Spatial Information Theory* (pp 301–15) Springer, Berlin, Heidelberg

Lawton, CA (1996) Strategies for indoor wayfinding: The role of orientation, *Journal of Environmental Psychology*, **16** (2) pp 137–45

Lawton, CA and Kallai, J (2002) Gender differences in wayfinding strategies and anxiety about wayfinding: A cross-cultural comparison, *Sex Roles*, **47** (9) pp 389–401

Lawton, CA (2010) Gender, spatial abilities, and wayfinding. In *Handbook of Gender Research in Psychology* (pp 317–41) Springer, New York, NY

Løvs, GG (1998) Models of wayfinding in emergency evacuations, *European Journal of Operational Research*, **105** (3) pp 371–89

Mackett, RL (2021) Mental health and wayfinding, *Transportation Research Part F: Traffic Psychology and Behaviour*, **81** pp 342–54

Myers, M (2010) 'Walk with me, talk with me': The art of conversive wayfinding, *Visual Studies*, **25** (1) pp 59–68

Parasuraman, A, Ball, J, Aksoy, L, Keiningham, TL and Zaki, M (2020) More than a feeling? Toward a theory of customer delight, *Journal of Service Management*, **32** (1) pp 1–26

Passini, R (1981) Wayfinding: A conceptual framework, *Urban Ecology*, **5** (1) pp 17–31

Passini, R (1996) Wayfinding design: Logic, application and some thoughts on universality, *Design Studies*, **17** (3) pp 319–31

Prestopnik, JL and Roskos–Ewoldsen, B (2000) The relations among wayfinding strategy use, sense of direction, sex, familiarity, and wayfinding ability, *Journal of Environmental Psychology*, **20** (2) pp 177–91

Raubal, M and Egenhofer, MJ (1998) Comparing the complexity of wayfinding tasks in built environments, *Environment and Planning B: Planning and Design*, **25** (6) pp 895–913

Schwering, A, Krukar, J, Li, R, Anacta, VJ and Fuest, S (2017) Wayfinding through orientation, *Spatial Cognition & Computation*, **17** (4) pp 273–303

Timpf, S, Volta, GS, Pollock, DW and Egenhofer, MJ (1992) A conceptual model of wayfinding using multiple levels of abstraction. In *Theories and Methods of Spatio-Temporal Reasoning in Geographic Space* (pp 348–67) Springer, Berlin, Heidelberg

Timpf, S (2002) Ontologies of Wayfinding: A traveler's perspective, *Networks and Spatial Economics*, **2** (1) pp 9–33

Wiener, JM, Büchner, SJ and Hölscher, C (2009) Taxonomy of human wayfinding tasks: A knowledge-based approach, *Spatial Cognition & Computation*, 9 (2) pp 152–65

Woollett, K and Maguire, EA (2010) The effect of navigational expertise on wayfinding in new environments, *Journal of Environmental Psychology*, 30 (4) pp 565–73

Appendix G
Participatory action research

Participatory action research is a qualitative method of inquiry. The following resources provide a stepping-off point for deeper exploration of participatory action research. This is not intended to be a complete list of relevant sources. It is, however, a representative sample of the resources that have helped to shape my thinking in the current research.

Books

Participatory Research for Health and Social Well-Being, Tineke Abma, Sarah Banks, Tina Cook, Sonia Dias, Wendy Madsen, Jane Springett, Michael T Wright

Participatory Action Research: Theory and methods for engaged inquiry, Jacques M Chevalier and Daniel J Buckles

New Approaches to Qualitative Research: Wisdom and uncertainty, Maggie Savin-Baden and Claire Howell Major

How to Think Like an Anthropologist, Matthew Engelke

Ethnographic Thinking: From method to mindset, Jay Hasbrouck

Narrative Analysis: Qualitative research methods series 30, Catherine Kohler Riessman

Community-based Qualitative Research: Approaches for education and the social sciences, Laura Ruth Johnson

Relevant academic articles

Borda, OF, Reason, P and Bradbury, H (2006) Participatory (action) research in social theory: Origins and challenges. In *The Sage Handbook of Action Research: Participative inquiry and practice* , Sage, pp 27–37

Kemmis, S (2006) Participatory action research and the public sphere, *Educational Action Research*, **14** (4) pp 459–76

Khanlou, N and Peter, E (2005) Participatory action research: Considerations for ethical review, *Social Science & Medicine*, **60** (10) pp 2333–2340

Kidd, SA and Kral, MJ (2005) Practicing participatory action research, *Journal of Counseling Psychology*, **52** (2) p 187

Kindon, S, Pain, R and Kesby, M (2007) Participatory action research: Origins, approaches and methods. In *Participatory Action Research Approaches and Methods* (pp 35–44) Routledge

McTaggart, R (1991) Principles for participatory action research, *Adult Education Quarterly*, **41** (3) pp 168–87

McTaggart, R (1994) Participatory action research: Issues in theory and practice, *Educational Action Research*, **2** (3) pp 313–37

Ozanne, JL and Saatcioglu, B (2008) Participatory action research, *Journal of Consumer Research*, **35** (3) pp 423–39

Swantz, ML (2008) Participatory action research as practice. In *The Sage Handbook of Action Research: Participative inquiry and practice*, pp 31–48

Appendix H
Stop, ask and further exploration

I wrote this book as a means to share what I've learned so far about "stuckness" at points of uncertain transition. I also wanted to share the benefits of thinking about them before they happen as a means of preparing ourselves to have confidence in our ability to navigate them well when they come along—and they always come along. In some ways I view the contents of these chapters as a tribute to honor the amazing individuals, teams and organizations I've engaged with so far.

But this inquiry is far from over.

The work presented here barely scratches the surface of what we need to learn—in theory and in practice—about what it takes to navigate unrelenting change and how we best prepare ourselves and others to do it in a way that focuses on wellbeing and flourishing. For that reason, I view this as a work in progress. A conversation starter. A prompt to inspire, equip and encourage people to view top-of-mind issues like the future of work, the future of education, the future of culture, the future of the planet and where technology is taking us as a species and a planet through a creative problem-solving and wayfinding lens.

It is my hope that the work will inspire curiosity in you, the reader, and that some of you will join me on this journey of asking deeper questions and pursuing insights through empirical research and field engagements. You can find more information about ongoing projects and opportunities to connect on my website, www.stopaskexplore.com, or connect with me on LinkedIn, Twitter or other socials @joanpball.

References

Introduction

Arnett, J (2000) Emerging adulthood: A theory of development from the late teens through the twenties, *American Psychologist*, [55](5), pp 469–480

Black, P (2020) Retirement Or A 'Third Act': What Will You Choose? Forbes, 27 April, https://www.forbes.com/sites/forbescoachescoun cil/2020/04/27/retirement-or-a-third-act-what-will-you-choose/?sh= 35d2f929200e (archived at https://perma.cc/4WUR-LW5Q)

Carnevale, A, Hanson, A and Gulish, A (2013) Failure to Launch: Structural Shift and the New Lost Generation, https://1gyhoq479ufd3yna29x7ubjn-wpengine.netdna-ssl.com/ wp-content/uploads/2014/11/FTL_ExecSum.pdf (archived at https:// perma.cc/ASU5-6Y9Z)

Frost, R (1915) The Road Not Taken, *The Atlantic Monthly*, August

Fry, R (2013) A rising share of young adults live in their parents' home, https://www.pewresearch.org/ social-trends/2013/08/01/a-rising-share-of-young-adults-live-in-their-parents-home/ (archived at https://perma.cc/7VJB-TJFJ)

McKee, R (1999) *Story: Substance, structure, style and the principles of screenwriting*, Methuen Publishing, London

Robinson, O (2015) Emerging adulthood, early adulthood and quarter-life crisis: Updating Erikson for the twenty-first century, in Žukauskiene, R (Ed.) *Emerging Adulthood in a European Context*, Routledge, New York

Williams, C (2004) The sandwich generation, *Perspectives on Labour and Income*, **16** (4), pp 7–14

Chapter 1

Bateson, M (1989) *Composing a Life*, Grove Press, New York

Chapter 2

Hartley, C and Phelps, E (2010) Changing fear: The neurocircuitry of emotion regulation, *Neuropsychopharmacology*, **35** (1), pp 136–46

Taleb, N (2014) *Antifragile: Things that gain from disorder,* Random House, New York

Ungar, M (2019) *Change Your World: The science of resilience and the true path to success*, Sutherland House, Toronto

Chapter 3

Lakoff, G (2006) Conceptual metaphor, in Geeraerts, D (Ed), *Cognitive Linguistics: Basic readings,* pp 185–238, Mouton de Gruyter, Berlin

Lakoff, G and Johnson, M (1980) Conceptual metaphor in everyday language, *The Journal of Philosophy*, **77** (8), pp 453–86

Ries, E (2011) *The Lean Startup: how constant innovation creates radically successful businesses*, Portfolio Penguin, New York

Zaltman, G (2008) *Marketing Metaphoria: What deep metaphors reveal about the mind of consumers*, Harvard Business Press, Boston

Chapter 4

Hill, K (2011) Wayfinding and spatial reorientation by Nova Scotia deer hunters, *Environment and Behavior*, **45** (2), pp 267–82

Oldham, J (2015) The alternative DSM-5 model for personality disorders, *World Psychiatry*, **14** (2), pp 234–36

Savin-Baden, M (2008) *Learning Spaces: Creating opportunities for knowledge creation in academic life*, Open University Press, Maidenhead

Van Gennep, A (2019) *The Rites of Passage*, The University of Chicago Press, Chicago

Chapter 5

Eurich, T (2017) *Insight: Why we're not as self-aware as we think, and how seeing ourselves clearly helps us succeed at work and in life,* Penguin Random House, New York

Passini, R (1996) Wayfinding design: logic, application and some thoughts on universality, *Design Studies,* **17** (3), pp 319–31

Chapter 6

Luthans, F, Youssef, CM and Avolio, BJ (2015) *Psychological Capital and Beyond,* Oxford University Press, USA

Merril, R and McElhinny, M (1983) *The Earth's Magnetic Field: Its history, origin and planetary perspective,* Academic Press (International Geophysics Series, Volume 32), London and New York

Rand, K and Cheavens, J (2009) Hope Theory, in *The Oxford Handbook of Positive Psychology* (2nd ed), Oxford University Press, Oxford

Wiener, J, Schnee, A and Mallot, H (2004) Use and interaction of navigation strategies in regionalized environments, *Journal of Environmental Psychology,* **24** (4), pp 475–93

Chapter 8

Chevalier, J and Buckles, D (2013) *Participatory Action Research: Theory and methods for engaged inquiry,* Taylor and Francis, London

Chapter 9

Parasuraman, A, Ball, J, Aksoy, L, Keiningham, T and Zaki, M (2020) More than a feeling? Toward a theory of customer delight, *Journal of Service Management,* **32** (1), pp 1–26

Razumnikova, O (2013) Divergent Versus Convergent Thinking, in *Encyclopaedia of Creativity, Invention, Innovation and Entrepreneurship* (Ed Carayannis, E), Springer, New York

Chapter 11

Bateson, M (1989) *Composing a Life,* Grove Press, New York
Gatty, H (1999) *Finding Your Way Without Map or Compass,* Dover Publications, Mineola

Conclusion

Ruggeri, A (2018) Do we really live longer than our ancestors? BBC, 3 October, https://www.bbc.com/future/article/20181002-how-long-did-ancient-people-live-life-span-versus-longevity (archived at https://perma.cc/VMV2-F4T5)

Acknowledgments

This book would still be an ambition if it were not for the hundreds of people who allowed me to join them on their journeys into and through uncertain transitions and liminal spaces over the past 10 years. To the individuals, teams and organizations who I've worked with, thank you. The experiences you allowed me to share and the wisdom you uncovered inform the frameworks, approaches and tools in this book.

Many thanks to Aura Lehrer, Christine Anisko, Kim Gabelmann, Brittney Hiller, Stephanie Roth, Jody Weatherstone, Erika Simmons, Erica Buddington, Ashley Rigby, Tim Gilligan, Shireen Idroos, Tricia Douglas, Natalie Kuhn, Efrat Yardeni, Jamila Wallace, Erin Rech, Shikha Mittal, Matthew Politoski, Evan Dittig, Melissa Shaw Smith, Hannah Maxwell, Jordan Novak, Linda Mensch, Chelsea Simpson, Rebecca Pry, Elise Johansen, and Ava Burgos for all of the conversations and reflections. Your willingness to play in uncharted territory with me keeps me wondering and exploring.

I am so grateful to Kat Scimia (now Galbo!) for co-creating the earliest wayfinding workshops at St. John's University that eventually became the transition curriculum I use to support students transitioning from college to career. You, Winnie Li, Rachel Hoffman, Heidy Abdel Kerim, Kenzy Shetta, Ada Lee, Kristin Sluyk, Raquel Paul, Li Wanrong, Linyue Wang, and other former students helped me to see the need for this work and created the space for me to explore these questions at the earliest stages of this research.

On the editorial side, this book would not have been possible without writer, editor, teacher and creative coach Nancy Rawlinson. Nancy, your tireless reading, rereading and brilliant commentary on my proposal and manuscript helped me to make sense of what it was I hoped to say and to discern how best to share this work and remain true to my own voice. This project would not have seen the light of day without you.

My sincere gratitude to consultant, speaker and author, Tom Goodwin. Tom, your willingness to share my work with Kogan Page helped to facilitate a wonderful working relationship with Commissioning Editor Géraldine Collard. Thanks Géraldine for your kindness, your counsel and for driving a hard bargain on a tight deadline. I could not ask for a better team than you and my other collaborators at Kogan Page. Many thanks one and all.

I am ever so grateful to my Clubhouse community and the members of the Wayfinders Club, whose stories, insights and questions allowed me to flush out my ideas and bring the work to life when Covid had us all at home.

Special thanks to my dear friend Rebecca Taylor for the long walks, generous edits and kind encouragement in the dog days of tight deadlines, and to a.m. Bhatt for social rooms and smart conversation. aJAR will be up and running by the time this book is published and I cannot wait to see where we take it.

Finally, and most importantly, I would like to thank my family. Kelsey—your input, edits and willingness to experiment with me made my research more fun than research should be. I am so glad to have you as a daughter and a friend. My dear Ian, your energy, joy and countless hours of transcription management helped keep me on track and gave me joy when I was in the weeds. To Andrew, our conversations and rides on the Peloton were a breath of fresh air in the writing process. And to my dearest Martin. Thank you for the stunning graphics, for listening to countless hours of me thinking out loud about this work for the better part of a decade. Whether sitting across a table, chatting from the car, or over Zoom from so many writing retreats, your willingness to listen and provide feedback was instrumental to this book becoming what it is. I love you and am so grateful for the space we make for one another to bring our dreams to life.

About the author

Joan Ball is an associate professor of Marketing at St. John's University in New York City and the founder of WOMBLab, a transition services firm. Her research, teaching and consulting focus on the design of systems and processes for lifelong learning, social impact and human flourishing. She is particularly interested in ways individuals and organizations in transition might engage service design strategies, tools and techniques to gather and distribute resources to support inquiry, exploration and wayfinding. She lives in the Hudson Valley of New York with her husband Martin.

Disclosures

M any of the examples, insights and models I use in these pages emerged from my work with individuals, groups and organizations. Some of them are referred to by name in these pages. Others chose to share their stories using a pseudonym or without a name to maintain their anonymity. In all cases, permissions were granted to share stories and insights derived from research and practice.

Index

Page numbers in *italic* indicate figures

CPSIA information can be obtained
at www.ICGtesting.com
Printed in the USA
JSHW011244100622
26897JS00015B/117